THE
MAN'S
GUIDE
TO
WOMEN

THE MAN'S GUIDE TO WOMEN

Scientifically Proven Secrets from the "Love Lab" about What Women *Really* Want

John Gottman, PhD
Julie Schwartz Gottman, PhD
Douglas Abrams
Rachel Carlton Abrams, MD
with **Lara Love Hardin**

RODALE.

RODALE *wellness*

Live happy. Be healthy. Get inspired.

Sign up today to get exclusive access to our authors, exclusive bonuses,
and the most authoritative, useful, and cutting edge information on health,
wellness, fitness, and living your life to the fullest.
Visit us online at RodaleWellness.com
Join us at RodaleWellness.com/Join

© 2016 John Gottman, PhD, Julie Schwartz Gottman, PhD,
Douglas Abrams, and Rachel Carlton Abrams, MD

Rodale books may be purchased for business or promotional use or for special sales.
For information, please write to:
Special Markets Department, Rodale Inc., 733 Third Avenue, New York, NY 10017

Printed in the United States of America
Rodale Inc. makes every effort to use acid-free ♾, recycled paper ♻.

Illustrations on pages 94, 95, and 99 by Elsbeth Mumm
Part opener and Cheat Sheet icons © iStock/Getty Images Plus
Book design by Carol Angstadt

Library of Congress Cataloging-in-Publication Data is on file with the publisher.

ISBN 978-1-62336-184-6   hardcover

Distributed to the trade by Macmillan
8   10   9   hardcover

We inspire and enable people to improve their lives and the world around them.
rodalebooks.com

CONTENTS

Secrets from the Love Lab

THERE IS A vicious rumor going around that men don't buy books.

If you are a man and you bought this book (or borrowed it), congratulations! You are a pioneer. A stereotype-busting man among men. A soon-to-be Hero who knows how to be the man that all women wish they had. If your girlfriend or wife bought the book and left it on your nightstand, we say no harm, no foul. You did not put your own hard-earned money down for the book, but it will reward you nonetheless for any and all time you invest in it.

If you are a woman reading this book, we are glad you are. We can guess what your motivations might be. Perhaps you want to vet this guide for accuracy and then give it to the man in your life (and possibly also to your brother, son, friend, neighbor, or male pet; sorry, we can't help your pet). We want to reassure you that we've done the vetting for you, as this guide for men is coauthored by two highly qualified female clinicians who have done the checking under the hood.

We also want to speak up for the man in your life and let you in on one of his little secrets: In the vast enigmatic world that is Woman, he is dreadfully lost and confused, and as is the case with most men, loath to ask for directions. We're not being critical or disloyal. Men freely admit this. Women are mysterious. (Men, are we right?) Your man desperately wants to understand how to love

you, make you happy, and ensure that you will desire and want him (and only him) forever. He wants to fight with you less. He wants to play with you more. He wants to know how your brain works, what makes your heart beat faster, and how to be the kind of man you need him to be. So be reassured, and feel free to read this book as well. But then give it to the man in your life, or leave it underneath the remote, or in his car, or stuff it in his toolbox, if that's what it takes. Or you can encourage him to go out and bravely forge his own path to the bookstore and buy a copy for himself.

Now, for the men. We know some secrets, and we're going to share them with you. We've written this book as an easy-to-read and easy-to-use guide. We've also tried to write this book to be entertaining and whenever possible to include visuals and cartoons, since sometimes a picture is worth a thousand (or at least a few hundred) words. And who doesn't love a good cartoon?

So here's the news flash: Men, you have the power to make or break a relationship. That's right. Research shows that what men do in a relationship is, by a large margin, the crucial factor that separates a great relationship from a failed one. This does not mean that a woman doesn't need to do her part, but the data proves that a man's actions are the key variable that determines whether a relationship succeeds or fails, which is ironic, since most relationship books are written for women. That's kind of like doing open-heart surgery on the wrong patient.

So while you may lament that you don't know why women act the way *they* do, and think the way *they* do, and talk the way *they* do, and perhaps you even blame them for your lack of success with them—the truth is, it is what *you* do and the way *you* think that matters most. The bar stools of the world are filled with lonely men sitting in the rubble of their failed one-liners and wondering what's wrong with women. We don't want that same fate for you. We're not going to tell you what's wrong with women—we're going to explain where you may have gone wrong in the past. When it comes to women, men are either Zeros or Heroes. And we know which one you'd rather be.

Caveat emptor: This isn't a how-to guide for getting women into bed. There are plenty of those, and most of them are based on shallow scams that do not lead to any kind of lasting or fulfilling relationship. This book will certainly help you seduce and satisfy women, but our goal is to help you succeed with women for a lifetime. All of the research studies show that men who are in happy, healthy relationships make more money, have more sex (yes, believe it or not, married men typically have much more and better sex than single men), live longer, suffer less chronic illness, and show less cognitive impairment—i.e., don't lose their minds—in their later years. So feel free to use this book to get a woman into your bed by skipping right to the chapters on romancing and making love to a woman. But if you want to keep her, and not spend your old age alone and doddering around the neighborhood in utter confusion, read the chapters on understanding a woman's mind, and heart, and the chapter on loving her for a lifetime.

It would be easy if there were a sequence of buttons to push to win the heart of any woman, but there's not. Women are complex. Every woman is different, and that's why every woman is so fascinating. This book will help you to understand how to dial out the static and confusion that so frequently becomes the backdrop to a relationship. We know what matters most to women and what women want most from a man. Read this guide, and we promise that you will be able to dial in a more satisfying relationship for yourself and for her.

How Do We Know?

John Gottman, PhD, is the guy who is known for being able to predict with 94 percent accuracy whether a couple will get divorced. The scientific laboratory is his major source of knowledge.

John is a researcher, and his wife, Julie Schwartz Gottman, PhD, is a clinical psychologist who has worked side by side with John to strengthen couples' relationships worldwide. Doug and Rachel are the coauthors of international, best-selling books about intimacy and passion, and Rachel is a physician who uses her clinical experience to help many women and men heal their hearts as well as their bodies in her medical practice.

In addition to being the world's leading marriage researcher, John has also distinguished himself by being in many disastrous relationships with women before he met Julie. We want to be perfectly clear on this point: His history with women is mostly a field littered with the corpses of failed relationships. Doug was not born a Don Juan either, although he did eventually write a novel about the famous seducer, and that book has been translated and read all around the world.

So if neither John nor Doug were born blessed with a secret knowledge of women, how have they managed to stay married to amazing women for almost 30 and 29 years, respectively?

It can't be stated enough: These two are not any kind of love gurus. Everything they know about women they've had to learn the hard way, and in John's case, from over 40 years of studying real-life couples.

The guidance in this book comes from real-life research and real-life relationships—some bad, some good enough, and some great. A lot of this information is new to the clinical world. In the past, clinicians who wrote about relationships had only seen troubled couples, so they relied on their fantasies of what good relationships looked like. They didn't know how men in really great, happy relationships actually treated their partners. We do.

They didn't have the Love Lab.

We do.

Inside the Lab

In a small apartment laboratory at the University of Washington, in what came to be called the "Love Lab" by the media, John (and later Julie) used many different methods to study couples. For example, he videotaped them talking about how their days went after they'd been apart for at least 8 hours, he watched them argue, he watched them talk about pleasant topics, and he watched them spend whole days together in this small apartment. As they discussed the events of their days or conflicts between them, he measured how fast their hearts were beating, how fast their blood was flowing, how they were breathing, how much they were sweating, and how much they jiggled in their seats as they talked, all synchronized to a video time code. He had them watch their videotape and tell him what they were feeling, and sometimes he had them watch the tape again and try to guess what their partner was feeling.

He coded, one hundredth of a second by one hundredth of a second, their facial expressions, tone of voice, words, gestures, positive emotions (like interest, affection, humor, and understanding), and negative emotions (like disappointment, hurt, anger, and sadness). He also recorded their criticism, contempt, defensiveness, stonewalling, and many, many other interactions.

Then he interviewed each couple about the history and philosophy of their relationship. He interviewed each individual about his or her own emotional history with anger, sadness, and fear.

Following all this assessment, he waited 1 to 3 years and then he saw them again. Then again, and again. He and Julie have now followed couples for as long as 20 years, throughout the course of their lives, through the newlywed years, through parenting, through aging. They have followed couples through midlife, retirement, and beyond—some even into their late eighties.

They've seen happy couples in all kinds of relationships, and they've seen unhappy couples break up or stay together in misery. Some of these couples wanted very interconnected, intimate relationships. Some wanted more independence from each other and more separation. Some couples fought a lot, and some avoided conflict entirely.

For 40 years, they've watched more than 3,000 couples, and these real couples taught them everything they know about who men and women are in relationships, and what women really want out of those relationships. In short, the secrets from the Love Lab are the secrets that every man needs to know, and these are the secrets that will make sure you are a Hero, not a Zero.

Now it's time for men to roll up their sleeves and understand what it is women want and need from them, how best to provide it, and what it takes to be in a happy, loving relationship with a woman for a lifetime. In this book, we will show you the secrets of attraction, of dating, of mating, and of day-to-day living with a woman. We will map her body and decode her body language. And the best way to begin is to start right at the heart of the matter and tell you the number one thing women want from a man.

THE MAN'S GUIDE

PART ONE

TO WOMEN

Understanding a Woman

Chapter 1

WHAT DO WOMEN REALLY WANT?

Understanding the Heart of a Woman

*The great question that has never been answered
and which I have not yet been able to answer, despite
my 30 years of research into the feminine soul, is
"What does a woman want?"*

−Sigmund Freud

*Trying to understand women is like
trying to smell the color nine.*

−Will Ferrell

STEPHEN HAWKING, the legendary astrophysicist and a man who has solved some of the most complex mysteries of the universe, was recently asked what it is he thinks about most. His answer came as no surprise to us. Which scientific puzzle confounds the genius of Hawking? "Women," he said. "They are a complete mystery."

If Hawking, Freud, and Ferrell, two of the greatest scientists and one of the funniest comics of our time, can't understand women, what hope is there for the average guy? How is he to muddle through the perplexing universe that is Woman? The first thing you need to know in order to unravel this mystery is simple: All women are unique. That's right, every last one of them is special. Ultimately, the goal is not to become the world's greatest lover, or boyfriend, or husband, but to become the world's greatest lover, boyfriend, or husband of your particular partner. In short, where your woman's wants and needs contradict the data from our lab, listen to your partner. Her truth is really the only truth that matters. Yet this book will help you accelerate the learning curve, because our research also reveals that women possess aspects in common in how they play, work, dream, and love, and those are the secrets we want to share with you. The second thing you need to know is that it is not as complicated as you think.

Imagine you are a tourist in a foreign land, and this book is your guided tour of the heart and mind—and, oh yeah, body—of that sovereign state. Like when visiting any foreign land, you want to be prepared—read the travel advisories, pack the right

©Clipartof.com

equipment, study the language, and learn as much as you can about the culture, the history, and the customs. Total immersion. You also want to learn the laws of the land; you should know what constitutes a crime and what the penalties are. Think *Midnight Express*. No one wants to end up in prison in a foreign country. The *Land of Women* is no exception.

The One Thing All Women Look for in a Man

What is the number one thing that women are looking for in a man? Six-pack abs? Six-figure bank account? A tall, handsome man riding a white horse? No, no, and no. The number one thing women look for is simply this: trustworthiness. That's right, trustworthiness. Now before you go patting yourself on the back and putting this book down because you know that she knows that you are trustworthy, think again. Trustworthiness isn't just about whether or not you are a player or, if you're in a long-term relationship, whether or not you've ever been unfaithful. Although those things are fundamental and important to trust-worthiness, they are not enough.

What trustworthiness looks like in dating and mating is this: You are who you say you are and you do what you say you are going to do. It's about reliability, accountability, and showing up just as you are (but with good hygiene). Why is trustworthiness so important? Why is this the quality that makes a woman's heart soar? Think about it. Throughout history, a woman's safety and well-being, as well as that of her children, have been dependent on her partner's trustworthiness. This is not just some antiquated issue from yesteryear, either. Fathers turn out to be the most critical factor in the health and success of children across a wide range of influences. When fathers are not involved with their kids, there's a five times greater likelihood that the kids will live in poverty, a three times greater likelihood that they'll fail in school, and a two times greater likelihood that they will have emotional and behavioral problems, use drugs, get involved in crime, or commit suicide.[1] Men make a difference. And men matter immensely to women and to their children, so there's a reason women are looking for men who are trustworthy.

Now you may be saying, "Hold on a minute, we've just met" or "I'm just looking for a date." Well, knowing what her deep, evolutionary needs are will help you know how to win her heart for a night or for a lifetime. Just remember that she's asking herself, even if she's not consciously thinking about it, "Is he safe? Will he be there for me? Is he dependable? Is he trustworthy?" There is a reason that women think that firefighters are hot. (And it's not the moustaches.) They are a symbol of all of these qualities. Firefighters are Heroes. You can be, too.

This is why all of those symbolic actions of concern and protectiveness that your grandmother told you to do are actually so important. Opening a door for her, pulling out her chair, and walking on the traffic side of the street (yeah, really) all signal that you care about her and are willing to protect her. By showing up on time and doing what you say you'll do, you tell her, "Hey, you can trust me." People admire it or dismiss it as being chivalrous, but the truth is, you're just signaling that you are trustworthy.

But being trustworthy is not just about safeguarding a woman's body or her children. It's about safeguarding her heart, as well.

The Two Major Complaints That Women Have

In our Love Lab, we found that women have two major complaints about men. The first complaint is: "He is never there for me." The second complaint is: "There isn't enough intimacy and connection." These women feel alone even when they are in a relationship.

In many ways, these are related complaints. These women cannot trust their men to be there for them when they need them. Most of the time, this is about being there for them emotionally: listening to them, caring for them, and safeguarding their hearts.

In contrast, men have two major complaints about women: "There's too much fighting, and there's not enough sex." Sound familiar? These men are also lonely even when they are in a relationship. We found that men actually want intimacy just as much as women, but they feel that intimacy when there's less fighting and more sex.

These separate complaints from men and women are, in fact, causally related and can be addressed through a simple skill we like to call *attunement*. When men "attune" to their women, there is less fighting, more frequent (and better) sex, and both men and women no longer feel so alone. It is also the skill that leads to genuine emotional connection, which in turn leads to trust, which in turn leads to you giving women the number one thing they need and want. In other words, this is a big deal.

In our interviews in the Love Lab, we asked men and women whether or not they felt they could talk to their partners (especially when they felt sad, angry, or in need of affection), and we discovered a fundamental fact: The fights of many couples result from men dismissing women's emotions instead of attuning to them. You dismiss a woman's emotions every time you try to fix them, distract her from them, minimize them, mock them, or ignore them altogether.

Learn the relatively simple and fundamental skill of attunement and your relationship with women will change profoundly. (Attunement will also serve you well at work, in parenting, and in all of your relationships.) We found that men who learned emotional attunement got what they ultimately wanted from their relationships: less fighting and more sex.

A Tune-Up

So why does this attunement thing work for your relationships with women? Women want men who are there for them when they need them. They want men who are interested in them and who care about them. Woman need to feel respected, heard, and connected. Now before you think, "blah, blah, blah," let's look at this as a logical equation.

Trait women want most: trustworthiness.

Trust is built through: emotional connection.

Emotional connection is created through: attunement.

Therefore, emotional attunement = trustworthiness.

So where can you buy a can of attunement? You can't. But you can learn it. It's not complex. It's not rocket science. And it has a handy acronym, so the next time you're with a woman you can think: Just A-TT-U-N-E.

ATTEND. Give your undivided attention when it's needed. This means that if a woman wants to talk to you, turn off the game, put away your cell phone, and show by your actions that you care about her and about what she is saying. Even if it is the minutiae of her day or something that seems unimportant to you, it is important to her and is a request for connection. If you are on a date, direct your attention to the woman you are with. No scanning the room, no checking out other women, no texting your buddies during dinner. Attention equals affection. Attention ultimately is how you express love.

TURN TOWARD. This is not a metaphor or a new age expression. Physically. Turn. Toward. Your. Partner. Women equate intimacy with conversation that is face-to-face and eyeball-to-eyeball. Biological anthropologist Helen Fisher, PhD, of Rutgers

University, says, "Men regard intimacy as playing or working side by side. Their approach to intimacy probably harks back to prehistory: Picture ancestral males gathering behind a bush, quietly staring across the grass in hopes of felling a passing buffalo. They faced their enemies but sat next to their friends."[2] Bottom line: Unless you and your woman are about to take down a buffalo, turn toward her while you talk.

UNDERSTAND. No matter what she is saying, the goal is understanding. And how you get to understanding is by asking questions. If the woman in your life is complaining about her best friend, don't offer a solution, don't try to distract her, don't think of how you can "fix" the problem, don't make jokes, and don't minimize the problem. Ask questions about what she is feeling and what it all means to her. This part of attuning is not about *saying* "I understand"; it's about *showing* genuine interest and attempting to understand *why* this is important to her. Whether she is complaining about her mother, frustrated with her boss, or pissed off at you—let understanding be your goal.

NONDEFENSIVELY LISTEN. If you are paying attention, turning toward her, and seeking understanding, you are well on your way down the path of nondefensive listening. This is especially important if what a woman is talking about or is upset about is *you*. Don't react. No one likes to be criticized or feel like they are under attack. But the tricky thing is, if you counterattack, make excuses, justify, or argue, you are only going to be criticized more. Don't interrupt and don't forget that any feeling is fact to the person feeling it. Whether or not you agree with her reactions or how she sees reality, her feelings are real to her in that moment. You only need to listen to her express them. You were given two ears and only one mouth for a reason—so you will listen twice as much as you speak. Many a wise man has followed these words. It's hard to underscore how important this finding was in our lab. The men who were able to "downregulate" their anger (in other words, calm themselves down and not overreact), were the men with great relationships.

EMPATHIZE. For you Trekkies out there, think of empathy as a Vulcan mind meld. For those of you thinking you've already covered this with the whole "understanding" thing, think again. Understanding is an intellectual pursuit, while empathy is an emotional pursuit. Try to feel how a woman is feeling, regardless of whether—in your opinion—it has any Vulcan logic to it. Clue in to the emotions she's expressing. How do you do this? You can ask her how she feels (genius). You can also read her body language. (Are her arms crossed, is her breathing shallow, is her face red? These are all signs she might be royally pissed off.) Let her know that you value how she feels and that it makes sense to you that she would feel this way. We won't go deep into the brain science explaining why this works, but let's just say that the emotional part of the brain calms down when it feels connected to another person and not alone. Show empathy. Show compassion. It's not about being wrong or being right.

If some part of you is screaming, "If I do this, she will roll right over me—she'll win!" remember that attuning with how she feels doesn't mean that you agree with everything that she says, just that you hear her—that you "get it." And we promise that if you do this first, your discussion about how you might solve the conflict between you will go *much* better (see Chapter 10). You will have less fighting and more sex. Because instead of being simply pissed off at you, she will feel *safe* and *heard,* and therefore interested in and willing to solve the problem between you so you can get on with the fun of being together.

Attuning is a skill, and like any skill, you get better with practice. So practice. Attune with your partner, attune with your mother, attune with your buddy, attune with your boss, attune with your dog.

This simple skill, this simple process, can profoundly change your interactions with all of the women in your life, and it changes the entire dynamic of dating and mating. Most men spend their time trying to impress women, talking and talking about themselves, and end up turning women off. This is the exact opposite of what women want. To put it simply, listening is sexier than talking. Asking questions is sexier than broadcasting. Being genuinely interested *in her* is much more important than trying to be interesting *to her*.

As we've stated, if you want a relationship with a woman to last, she needs to know who you are, and she needs to feel safe with you. Emotional safety, like emotional connection, is built through the process of attuning. When a woman makes a bid for your attention, when she reaches out to you emotionally and you meet her reach, this demonstrates your trustworthiness and emotional safety. If you shut her down, ignore her, or otherwise don't attune (especially when she is upset), she will not feel safe with you emotionally, nor will she feel safe to be herself with you.

A woman also needs physical safety. Everyone learned in kindergarten that it's not okay to hit someone, but there are other, less obvious ways that a woman can feel physically unsafe with you. Men are often bigger than women and their voices are deeper and louder. If you use your voice or your size to intimidate or to make a point, even if you don't intend to do this, a woman will not feel physically safe with you and will not trust you completely. You can attune all day and night, but you will never obtain Hero status in the trustworthy department if you lead with your might.

I'll Do That Trustworthiness Thing When I'm Married

Perhaps you aren't in a long-term relationship with a woman, and perhaps you have no desire to be in a long-term relationship with a woman. The trustworthiness factor is the same. Even if you are dating 10 different women you met online, there still has to be a level of trust if you want a great sex life, a fun dating life, or to have an overall good time.

For women, being sexual is equivalent to being vulnerable. And nothing will stop arousal in its tracks or reverse it more quickly than fear. We're not talking about the fear that you are going to hurt her physically, although that's clearly a deal breaker. We're talking about the fear that you will hurt her emotionally. The fear that she is not safe with you. It's basic biology, and we will talk more about the fear center in a woman's brain in the next chapter. For now, it is enough to know that if she thinks you are lying to her, being fake, not being accountable, dismissing her feelings, or just not showing up to the party in some way—your sex life will suck. And no man wants that.

What Do Men Want?

We've already defined from our research what it is men want: less fighting and more sex. But in a more general way, a man wants to be desired and to feel like the woman in his life wants him, adores him, and approves of him just the way he is. It's no secret. You know this is true. You want approval from the women in your life. Actually, you want approval from all of the women in the world, but for now let's settle on helping you get it from the woman or women closest to you, and then you can work on conquering the rest of the world.

Men also want less conflict. Way less conflict. You don't want to be the source of her unhappiness, and when she's unhappy, you want to fix whatever's broken and move on. Men feel responsible for women's feelings. And this is where men go way, way wrong.

Women have big feelings. Men have big feelings, too, but they're better at hiding them. And when women have big feelings, men want to jump in and make those feelings go away. Be honest—

sometimes the big feelings of women scare the crap out of you. Nothing can send a grown man into a panic faster than tears that seem to come out of nowhere, make no logical sense, and call for a 2-hour "talk" to make them subside. You want to immediately get to the source of the problem, but this is not how women work.

John saw a couple in therapy who struggled with this issue. The man said that whenever his wife came into a room he tensed up and scanned her body to see if there was any evidence of her being in a dark mood. He came to therapy wanting John to determine if there was something mentally wrong with his wife. The woman said that whenever she walked into a room he became like the Batmobile: The shields came up immediately, making him invulnerable, impenetrable. There was no way she could get close to him. She claimed he never listened to her. "You are never there for me when I need you," she said. He claimed that he listened to her all the time.

As John observed the couple together, it became clear that the man's attitude toward her emotions was impatience; he had a kind of "What is it now?" attitude. He was irritable. As he listened to her, he saw himself as responsible for changing her negative, unhappy state to a more positive, optimistic one. He believed his role as her husband was to *make* her happy, so when she was unhappy he would suggest a way that he could solve the problem, and he'd offer how he would choose to feel if he were in the same situation.

Sound logical?

Big mistake.

The man was full of what he saw as sage advice, like, "When the world deals you a bad hand, you just play the hand you are dealt." The advice did nothing to help his wife feel listened to. On the contrary, it made her feel that he thought she was stupid to be distressed at all, so she felt humiliated for having been so emotional.

What could this man have done differently? How could he have been there for her? Demonstrated his trustworthiness? It goes back to attunement. It always goes back to attunement. He needed to Attend-in other words, pay Attention to his wife. He needed to Turn Toward her. He needed to Understand. He needed to Nondefensively Listen. He needed to Empathize. He didn't need to problem solve. He didn't need to philosophize. He didn't need to personalize. He didn't need to fix her or her emotions or her supposed "mental problems." He just needed to know that she wanted to feel less alone.

Knowing these insights is a big relief, because it means you're actually under a lot less pressure. And the payoff is huge. When you attune, the woman you're with feels safe. When she feels safe, the world is your oyster and life is good. Sex is good. Your relationship is playful and happy and joyous.

If you are in a close relationship with a woman, you are going to get to see *all* of her emotions (and all of your own emotions) in their raw, ugly beauty. Don't let them scare you. Don't think you can give her logical reasons why they should not be present. Acceptance is the key. As you learn to accept her emotions, you may learn to accept your own. Women often have stronger emotions than men; there's a hormonal basis to this difference. You can see these emotional differences between the sexes in childhood play. To understand this, let's take a look at the games John observed children playing at recess on the playground.

Learn from the Children

First, let's watch the 8-year-old boys. Boys at this age tend to play run and chase games with a ball. An example is a made-up game called Mob. One boy would get the ball and it was the job of about 30 other boys to chase him as a group and take the ball away from him in any way they could. Once "mobbed," the boy would either hang on to the ball or pass it to a friend, who then became "it" and the subject of the chase. The boys needed a large area to play this game. The main activity was running like hell.

They were very serious about the game, but there was also a lot of laughter. But once in a while a boy got overly emotional. Most of the time the kids just ignored this disruption and kept playing the game, hoping it would work itself out. But sometimes the boys would deal directly with the emotion. For example, one day a kid named Brian started to cry, loudly. Another kid, Gabe, who was sort of the self-appointed captain of this semiorganized chaos, stopped everyone by shouting, "Hey everyone! Stop!" and went over to Brian. "What's the matter?" he asked. Brian, through his tears, said, "I never get the ball." Gabe then shouted to the other kids, "Let's go! Only this time Brian gets the ball. Here's the ball. Okay, you're it, Brian. Let's go!"

And they were off. Problem solved. Emotions dealt with. The goal of the boys was to keep the ball in play no matter what the cost. Emotions just got in the way of the game. Crying was like an unwelcome leech that had landed on someone and was messing up the fun. The goal was to get rid of the leech and continue the play. This seems to be true of males whether they are 8 or 48. The goal for men is generally dispensing with the emotion so that the play and fun (relationship) can continue.

Now, let's observe the 8-year-old girls on the same playground.

Lisa and Kathy are playing hopscotch when Kathy starts to cry. "What's wrong?" asks Lisa. "You hurt my feelings," says Kathy. "How did I do that?" asks Lisa. Kathy explains that she wanted Lisa to wear the same barrette in her hair that Kathy had on, and she had brought an extra one from home especially for Lisa. She was hoping that Lisa would wear it as a sign that they were best friends. Lisa says she doesn't like to wear barrettes in her hair. Kathy cries harder. "But I do want to be best friends," says Lisa.

It doesn't stop there. The girls go on to review how they first met and how they became friends. They talk about doing a sleepover, plan whose house it is going to be at, and discuss what they might do together during the sleepover. They decide to one day marry brothers, so they can become sisters. This goes on and on. The game of hopscotch is long forgotten. It is only a context for the relationship. And emotions are a way of getting closer. They are the stuff of intimacy, and that's the real reason the girls play the game: The feeling of connection with one another. The actual game is okay, but it's often just a mask for exploring the closeness of the relationship.

For the girls, the goal isn't the game and stopping the play isn't a drawback or a disruption of the fun. Emotions are not a problem for girls. They are a good thing, an opportunity for intimacy. To girls, expressing the feelings requires taking a risk, opening up, and trusting one another. It's a good sign that the relationship is deepening. Eventually, Kathy and Lisa may solve the barrette problem. Lisa may agree to keep the barrette in her pocket. But the solution, if they ever determine one, is not even important.

The Bottom Line

Men are always asking the question, "What are women trying to accomplish when they become emotional?" This is a hopelessly male question. Women are baffled by this question. When men say a woman is being "emotional," they are not talking about joy, fun, play, humor, interest, excitement, adventure, lust, or passion. They are not talking about the positive emotions. Men have no problem with a woman expressing *those* emotions.

Men have a problem with the so-called "negative" emotions, like sadness, anger, fear, disappointment, jealousy, loneliness, shame, and insecurity. These are emotions that many men would just rather not have at all, much less constantly talk about or dwell on. The majority of men believe that talking about these feelings will only make matters worse. This is not true.

But most women don't feel that way about these emotions. Let's be clear. Let's get to the ultimate bottom line: For a woman, there are no *negative* emotions. For a woman, there is no "point" to being emotional. Emotions just are. For women, they're as natural as breathing.

Emotions are opportunities for intimacy. This bears repeating. They are opportunities to build emotional connection, and they are opportunities to demonstrate your trustworthiness.

Ultimately, any relationship between two people will have "issues." No two people are going to agree on everything. The goal is not to turn the other person into you. The goal is to understand the unique, amazing, annoying, complex, frustrating, fascinating person you are in a relationship with. Wouldn't it be boring if you were dating a clone of yourself, or worse, married to your clone? Since you can't clone yourself what can you do? You can try to understand her. When you give up trying to change her into someone more like you, you can attune to who she really is. That's when the real magic happens.

When in doubt, remember the hopscotch story. Put a barrette in your hair and show up and attune when your woman needs you. This is what it means to understand the heart of a woman.

CHEAT SHEET
for HEROES

★ **WHAT WOMEN WANT MOST: TRUSTWORTHINESS.** The number one thing women want from you is trustworthiness. You demonstrate trustworthiness by being who you say you are and doing what you say you are going to do. You show up and you show up as yourself.

★ **THE SECRET OF TRUSTWORTHINESS: ATTUNEMENT.** Women need to feel emotionally connected and emotionally safe. This happens through attunement. When a woman wants to connect with you, especially when she's upset about something, you A-TT-U-N-E: You Attend to her, you physically Turn Toward her, you seek to Understand her by asking questions, you Nondefensively Listen, and you Empathize by accepting and affirming her emotions.

★ **DON'T BEAT YOUR CHEST.** Women also need to feel physically safe with you. A Hero never uses his size or his voice to intimidate a woman or make a point. A lack of physical safety is a deal breaker with women.

★ **TRUSTWORTHINESS = LESS FIGHTING AND MORE SEX.** When a woman feels emotionally connected to you and when you demonstrate your trustworthiness, the result is less fighting and more sex. Win-Win-WIN.

YOU MIGHT BE A ZERO IF. . .

✖ You dismiss her emotions or immediately try to fix them.

✖ You use your voice, size, or strength to intimidate.

✖ You check your e-mail while she's trying to talk to you or in other ways that don't give her your attention when she needs it or asks for it.

✖ You don't show up when you say you will.

✖ You check out other women when you are with her.

✖ You keep secrets.

✖ You lie.

✖ You cheat.

✖ You lie about cheating.

Chapter 2

A MIND OF HER OWN

The Art of Understanding a Woman's Brain

LET'S BE CLEAR right off the bat—we're not going to reinforce any stereotypes that are out there regarding the male brain and the female brain. You know the ones we are talking about.

If you were to come across two brains (it could happen) and pick each of them up in your hands, there would be no way to tell the gender of either brain. One would not be blue and the other pink. One would not be made of slugs and snails and puppy dog tails, and the other of sugar and spice and everything nice. Male *and* female brains both are made up of three main parts—the cerebrum, the cerebellum, and the brain stem. An adult brain (of either gender) consists of about 100 billion neurons connecting at 100 trillion points. Now, male brains tend to be 10 percent bigger than female brains, but don't let this serve as proof of any difference in gender intelligence. Male hands are about 10 percent bigger than female hands. Male torsos are about 10 percent bigger. For the most part, males are bigger than females, and the brain is no exception.

As far as intelligence is concerned, brain size does not matter. So while we've established that the brain of a woman has the same parts as the brain of a man, it does operate somewhat differently in two important areas: rhythm and fear. Grasp the importance of these two areas and you are going to get your Hero badge for understanding a woman's brain.

Rhythm

All human and mammalian bodies are rhythmic in many ways. We breathe rhythmically, our hearts beat rhythmically, our walking strides are rhythmic, our brain waves are rhythmic, our sleep-wake cycles are rhythmic, and much of our endocrine (hormone) systems are rhythmic. However, women are more complicated rhythmically than men, as their hormone levels rise and fall during each month with their menstrual cycles.

That's right. We're going to talk about the menstrual cycle. Understand her menstrual cycle and the rhythms of a woman's hormones, and you will understand much of what makes her tick—and what ticks her off.

The holy trinity of female hormones—estrogen, progesterone, and testosterone—determines a woman's day-to-day reality: what she values; how outgoing or active she is; what her needs are; and what, when, and even who she desires. You read that correctly—testosterone, often called the male sex hormone, is an equally important hormone for women.

During the first 2 weeks of the menstrual cycle (when estrogen is peaking), women are friendlier, more talkative, more socially relaxed, calmer, and more emotionally sensitive. During the second 2 weeks of the menstrual cycle (when progesterone is peaking), women can be more irritable, more stressed, and less calm, plus they want to be alone more. They can also be more focused on their interior worlds and more creative. This is a general guideline and varies from woman to woman; it also changes as a woman gets older and goes through perimenopause and menopause.

"No, he's not holding the place up. His wife's sent him in to buy feminine hygiene products."

.NAF.

Many women experience an increase in irritability and insomnia in the perimenopause period (mid-forties to mid-fifties) that is exacerbated by stress. A Hero helps his perimenopausal partner take care of herself, get more sleep, and doesn't take her mood personally. A woman's needs and emotions can vary throughout her menstrual cycle, although the differences may be extreme for some women and barely noticeable for others. At ovulation, women may be more emotional and possibly more interested in sex, which we discuss in detail in the following section, "Sex and Hormones." It is common for women to experience more emotional sensitivity, irritability, stress, and sadness when progesterone levels start to drop just before menstruation—commonly referred to as PMS, or premenstrual syndrome. This can occur just for 1 day or can last for an unpleasant 2 full weeks before menstruation begins. These symptoms can include mild to quite severe depression and anxiety. There are also physical symptoms such as headaches, backaches, cramping, and bloating. There are helpful things women can do to minimize PMS, ranging from exercise, avoiding caffeine, and taking B vitamins, herbs, or progesterone to full treatment with antidepressant therapy. As a man, you can be helpful by listening to her feelings (which are real, PMS or not), avoiding the temptation of blaming PMS for her emotional state (trust us, this will *not* earn you points, whether it is true or not), and not trying to fix it. Need help? Here is a common response we've heard, and then a suggested rewrite:

WRONG	RIGHT
"Seems like every month or so you have yourself a pity party, and I say, 'Just get over yourself.' You've got it pretty easy, as I see it."	"Sounds to me like you're feeling really sad at the moment. Talk to me. I want to hear what you're thinking and feeling right now."

So although it is true that she might benefit from, say, less caffeine and more exercise, it would be better for your physical safety if you don't mention that. Enough said? Some women really crave alone time before menstruation. One way that you can support her having some solitude is by taking care of your shared responsibilities so she can have some time to herself. In traditional cultures, there was often a place where menstruating women could go to be alone during this time of the month, where they could be relieved of tasks and have time for introspection and reflection. This tradition has been lost in the modern world, but if you can support her as she navigates the emotional tides of her hormones, you will be a Hero among men.

Not every woman has a 28-day cycle (normal cycles can range from 20 to 40 days), and not every woman has the same PMS symptoms. General health, stress levels, and medications (including birth control pills) can also change a woman's cycle, including both its length and the emotional intensity experienced during it.

Bottom line: There's no set rule that applies to all women, and your best bet is to become familiar with the cycle and needs of the woman you're in a relationship with—while also knowing that all rules are subject to change without advance notice. What you need to remember is that the woman you were in a relationship with last week might not be the woman you are in a relationship with this week. The only constant is change. And the less you take her moods personally, the better off you will be. Believe it or not, her moods generally have nothing to do with you.

Hormones and Sex

Hormones have a much more dramatic effect on a woman's sex drive than most men realize. These hormonal peaks and valleys and cyclical changes in a woman's emotional state can alter her desire for, and receptiveness to, sex. As one telling example, women tend to be somewhat more attracted to aggressive (alpha) men when they are ovulating and more attracted to kinder, gentler, more nurturing (beta) men when they are not.

This may come from a natural cycle that has its evolutionary origins in women's long-standing needs to have children that were strong enough to survive—and to find men who would love and protect their children to make sure they would thrive. These are obviously not conscious choices, and women can certainly override these unconscious impulses, but it's important for men to know that they are not necessarily meeting the identical woman, in the living room or the bedroom, from day to day. And she does not want the identical man from day to day, either. Her needs, feelings, and thoughts may vary depending on where she is in her cycle.

It's also important to know that this fluctuating need for an alpha *and* a beta male at any given time does not mean a woman needs two different men. But it may mean that you need to adapt to and match the rhythm of her hormones and be both alpha and beta. This is what the Heroes do, the ones who know how to attune with their women not just emotionally, but physically, as well. She may want you to take a protector role one day, as the two of you are coming home late from a movie, and on another day, she might want you to take a nurturer role by cuddling up with her on the couch and talking about, you know, *feelings.*

No wonder men are so lost in the land of women.

Research has shown that men are aware of when a woman is ovulating, even if only unconsciously. A study published in the journal *Evolution & Human Behavior* tracked the tip money received from approximately 5,300 lap dances given by women in strip clubs.[1] The dancers logged their menstrual cycles, their work hours, and their tip money, and it turned out that the dancers made 80 percent more money in tips when they were ovulating. They received the least amount of money when they were menstruating. And what's really fascinating: Women who were on the Pill had no change in the amount of tips they received. (Women who are on the Pill do not ovulate at all and their hormones remain relatively constant.) It seems women aren't the only ones driven by the hormonal changes associated with ovulation.

Whether the men were unconsciously picking up on the women's ovulation or the women's ovulation was causing them to perform moves that increased their tips, there's more going on below the surface than you realize. Many couples report an increased intensity to their lovemaking during ovulation, but women are by no means only aroused during ovulation. Unlike other primates, humans don't go into "estrous" (heat), and many women are just as horny at other times in their cycle, including when they are menstruating. It should be noted that many woman have a hormonally influenced drop in sex drive with menopause, though this is by no means across the board. The good news is that women (as long as they're getting help with vaginal dryness—a little topical estrogen goes a long way) enjoy sex just as much after menopause as before. They just may need a bit more coaxing to get there.

Another important hormone to be aware of is testosterone. And as we mentioned previously, testosterone is not the sole property of men. It is actually the engine of sexual desire in both men and women, but men have on average 10 to 100 times more testosterone than women do.

Men's brain centers for sex (found in the hypothalamus) are twice as big as the sex centers in women, and indeed most men think about sex about six times more often than women do. As comedian Billy Crystal once said, "Women need a reason for sex. Men just need a place." And although in general men have stronger sex drives than women, this is by no means the rule. There are plenty of couples where the woman's desire for sex is equal to or greater than her partner's drive—and this is also normal.

In men, the brain centers for sex and for vision are closely linked, which is why just looking at women turns men on. And although women appreciate an attractive man, how a guy looks is not necessarily the reason a woman is attracted to him. We will discuss this more in Chapter 5, where we get into the science of seduction.

It is also the case that testosterone levels are higher in men during adolescence and young adulthood and, consequently, the sex drive peaks at those ages. For women, the sex drive doesn't peak until the thirties, making for interesting challenges and opportunities as long-term relationships mature. Men and women often find that their sex drives align more closely as they enter their forties and fifties.

Women and Fear

Lynn and Mike are both in their fifties, married for more than 20 years, and full of stories about the ups and downs of their relationship and marriage. They had struggled with meeting the demands of a blended family, balancing two busy careers, and negotiating financial issues that always seemed to come up. Often, during the course of their marriage, it seemed as if they just didn't understand each other. They struggled to find their roles as a man and a woman, a husband and a wife. Lynn believed she and Mike couldn't grasp each other's way of viewing the world. "It was like we spoke a different language, and you know how when you are speaking to someone who doesn't understand English you end up yelling really loudly, thinking that will make the other person understand your language? It was like that for us. We were each speaking a foreign language and yelling louder and louder in hopes that the other person would magically understand and start speaking our language." Lynn goes on to add, "The problem was that I was trying to relate to Mike as if he were female—a big, hairy female—and I think he thought of me as a weaker, punier version of a man. We were stuck."

Both Lynn and Mike were frustrated by a marriage that seemed to have turned more into a weird form of competitive living than a partnership. In desperation, Lynn grabbed Mike and brought him to a workshop about understanding women. Mike felt like he had been trying to understand Lynn for decades, but he went along for the ride. He imagined the person teaching the workshop would decipher the code or explain to him why women just couldn't think rationally, like men do.

The woman who was leading the workshop began by asking one question: "This is for the men, first. How many of you have ever feared for your life or your physical well-being?" After a long pause, a few of the 50 men in the room raised a hand. "When was the last time you feared for your life or your physical well-being?" There was an awkward silence for a bit, but eventually the men started raising their hands to answer.

"Well, there was this one time way back in high school when I got into a fist fight," one man explained.

Another said, "Once, about 10 years ago, when I had too much to drink and ended up in a really bad neighborhood in Los Angeles. It was just for a moment."

"In Vietnam," said a third, who was a veteran.

As each of the men answered, it became clear that the awkward silence wasn't about feeling uncomfortable answering the question, it was because they were struggling to remember a time when they felt fear for their safety. All of the examples the men gave were from 10, 20, 30, or more years in the past.

Next she asked the women. "How many of you have ever been afraid for your life?" Every female hand in the room went into the air. "How many of you have been afraid in the last 6 months?" Again, every hand went in the air. "How about in the last month?" "The last week?" Every hand was raised. Finally she asked the question, "How many of you were nervous or fearful walking through the hotel parking garage to come to this workshop?" Again, every hand was raised, including Lynn's.

Mike was stunned. He had no idea Lynn experienced fear. He wasn't afraid, so he assumed she wasn't afraid. He thought about the times he had told her he would meet her in the car. The times he walked in front of her on the street when they were out. "That one example," explains Mike, "changed everything between us. I realized I had been assuming she viewed the world through the same lens I viewed the world through—and it was eye-opening."

Lynn was just as astounded that Mike hadn't felt fear for his physical well-being in 30 years. "It was one of those things that made us look at each other differently. What else didn't we know about each other? What else was there to learn?"

In that workshop, Mike learned something critically important about women—they experience fear in a very different way than men.

It is a sad reality that women feel more vulnerable in the world than men do—and by vulnerable, we don't just mean emotionally. In this case, we are talking physically. Another sad reality is that one out of four girls has been sexually abused by the age of 18, and that number is higher (just using logic makes this true) if you consider unreported cases. In Japan, women ride a special pink train that's just for them because they fear being groped. Fifty percent of women in the military have been raped or sexually assaulted in some way. Women are twice as likely to develop post-traumatic stress disorder (PTSD) after trauma as men are, which in turn leads them to be even more fearful in the future.

Women no doubt evolved this greater sensitivity to threatening situations in order to stay safe. It's hard to know how much is nature and how much is nurture, but we also live in a world that conditions women to feel afraid for their safety and well-being. Men are typically not conditioned this way. And because of this, men and women have huge differences in how they view fear, safety, and danger.

It is easy to demonstrate these sex differences in the psychology laboratory. The late Loren McCarter, PhD, a senior research analyst with the Behavioral Health Sciences Department, and his mentor, professor Robert Levenson, from University of California, Berkeley, conducted an experiment in which they fired off a gunshot behind their volunteer subjects. Levenson and McCarter were testing the startle reflex in men and women. Both genders had the same startle reflex, but different reactions to being startled. In general, men's heart rates went up much more than women's and took much longer to recover. The kicker to this study, however, was this: When they asked men and women what they were feeling after having been startled, women reported feeling afraid. Women felt fear. Men reported feeling angry, and some also had a desire to get even with the experimenter.[2]

Imagine you are driving in your car, about to take a woman out to dinner. A car cuts you off in traffic, coming incredibly close to hitting your front end. There is the initial startle both of you feel, but then you get pissed. You race up behind the driver of the other car and get as close as possible so he knows you are mad. Meanwhile, the woman next to you, who was also startled but felt fear rather than anger, is made even more fearful by your aggressive response to the other driver. What do you do? What does a Hero do in this instance? A Hero, realizing a woman's response to being startled is quite different than his own, backs off from the other driver and turns his attention to making the woman next to him feel safe.

What men need to know is that high stress causes men to get less fearful, but when women feel high stress they get more fearful and are more likely to be afraid in the future. Women are more likely to feel fear in response to a stressful situation than men are. Women also experience much more fear over the course of a lifetime, and once they feel fear in a situation, they will be even more afraid when that situation arises again in the future.

Think about this. Think about the women in that workshop Mike and Lynn attended who felt fear daily. This is the reality that women live in, and a deeper understanding of this can change not only your understanding of women but your relationships with them, as well. In the first chapter, we mentioned that women need to feel emotionally and physically safe with you. This isn't just good advice, it's advice based on their biological and physiological needs, which are different than yours.

In a critical study, University of Virginia psychologist James Coan, PhD, together with Hillary Schaefer, PhD, and Richard Davidson, PhD, monitored women in a functional MRI (magnetic resonance imaging) machine while they were subject to the threat of electric shock. In one set of experiments, each subject held her husband's hand; in another, each woman held the hand of an anonymous experimenter; and in a third, no one held the women's hands.[3]

When a happily married woman held her husband's hand, the fear response was completely shut down in her brain (specifically the amygdala, for you neuroscientists). When she held the hand of her husband but she didn't consider herself happily married, the fear response shut down a bit, but not all the way. When she held hands with a stranger, there was no change in her fear response. It was the same as when she held no one's hand.

These results show that your touch is very effective, and even holding hands can have a powerful effect on a woman.

So what are you to do, after learning how fear and fear conditioning work in a woman? Where do you begin?

For starters, when a woman is afraid, hold her hand.

Even better, try to help her avoid feeling afraid in the first place.

CHEAT ★ SHEET
for HEROES

★ **RHYTHMICITY.** Understand the effect of hormones on the day-to-day emotional state of a woman. Know that these influences are different in every woman and will change in a woman as she goes through different stages of her life. Her sex drive and what she needs from you will also change depending on where she is in her cycle. Ask questions to find out what she needs.

★ **FEAR.** Women experience fear differently than men. Women are more easily fear conditioned, meaning that if you both go through a fearful experience, she will be twice as likely to feel fear again in a similar situation. Offering comfort to a woman when she is afraid can immediately shut down her brain's fear response. That is, of course, assuming she's happy with you. If she's unhappy with you, your comfort may not be effective.

YOU MIGHT BE A ZERO IF. . .

✖ You ask her if she's having her period or "PMSing" when she is angry, emotional, or moody in some way.

✖ You dismiss her fear as irrational.

✖ You don't offer comfort when she is afraid or fearful.

✖ You grope her or engage in any unwanted sexual activity.

✖ You walk in front of her rather than behind or beside her when you are walking together on the street. There's a reason the codes of chivalry have a man walk on the outside: to protect his partner.

✖ You don't respect her physical or emotional vulnerability.

✖ You purposely frighten her because you think it's amusing (or because you now want to check out her startle response after reading about that study).

THE MAN'S GUIDE

PART TWO

TO WOMEN

Dating a Woman

Chapter 3

READ MY HIPS

Understanding Women and Attraction

JOHNATHAN SAT AT the head of the table. He spoke first, and then the other five people around him took turns speaking. When each was finished, they looked to him for approval. Every suggestion made was tentative until he validated that the course they were on was correct. He could think on his feet, strategize, and make decisions quickly and unequivocally. He held an erect and commanding posture. Anyone walking into the room would have no doubt that he was the person who held the power.

Sandra had gone out with Johnathan a few times. They were nice enough dates, but she hadn't felt a whole lot of chemistry between them. She had almost relegated him to the friend zone— but then she sat down at this table and watched him do what he did best. As she listened to him dispatch orders with confidence, fairness, and imagination, Sandra found herself, for the first time, incredibly attracted to him.

She felt the spark.

She saw him as the master of all he surveyed.

And it was around this particular table, during this particular game of Dungeons & Dragons, that Sandra began to fall in love with the man who would someday become her husband.

After all, who doesn't fall in love with the Dungeon Master?

Okay, so maybe you've never played Dungeons & Dragons, but you can embody the same qualities of the Dungeon Master that Sandra found so appealing. And what were the top qualities that attracted Sandra? Confidence, intelligence, and high social status. Now you might be wondering how being the Dungeon Master implies social status to anyone but a select group of role-playing nerds, but it does. Social status is contextual. In that context, Johnathan was the power broker; the commander in chief of the living room table. As Dungeon Master, he had the highest status in the room. In real life, he was a part-time barista and college student. But in that living room, in Sandra's eyes, he was nothing less than a Hero.

Mad Skills

Napoleon Dynamite had it somewhat right when he said, "Girls only want boyfriends who have great skills." Now you might not have nunchuck skills, bow hunting skills, or computer hacking skills, but whatever your skills, women will be attracted to the expertise you demonstrate in your particular area of interest. In other words, if you collect stamps, be the most powerful, high-status stamp collector there is. If you collect garbage, be the most fascinating, knowledgeable, and powerful garbage collector you can be. Women are attracted to men who are the CEO and president of. . . themselves.

We're not talking about arrogance, however. There is a big difference between confidence and arrogance. Confidence will attract a woman. Arrogance will repel her faster than you can say, "Help me shave my back." Confidence comes from being secure in your abilities. Arrogance actually comes from being insecure in your abilities.

Of course, before you can tell her about your wicked collection of vintage paint by number artwork, you have to get her to talk to you. And before you can get her to talk to you, you have to get her interested in talking to you. And before you can get her interested in talking to you, you have to get her to notice you exist on this planet of 7 billion people—of which 50.4 percent are men.

Sound like a lot of work?

It's not. But there's good news and bad news. The good news is that there are a few nonverbal cues you can send that will make you appear to be confident, intelligent, and high status. The bad news is that research shows that it's the woman who ultimately controls whether or not a man approaches her. That's right. You may think you have the best pickup lines invented since primitive men stopped using clubs, but those lines (like the earlier clubs) are virtually useless.

Now some men will want to automatically reject the research findings that show they are not exerting a supreme act of free will when they *choose* to approach a woman, but whether that approach happens at a dog park, bar, music festival, bookstore, or coffee shop, it is the woman who is giving your subconscious the cues that she is approachable and who beckons your "free will" into action.

Long before you decide to make your move, a woman has either given you the signals that she's interested or she's displayed disinterest. (These are the "you don't have a chance in hell" gestures.) Now some men choose to ignore the disinterested signals and approach regardless, and this is where the rejection happens. All men have their rejection statistics, but if you look closely at any given situation, the clues were probably there if the odds were against you.

A single woman will scan a room and instantly (and often subconsciously) determine which males are attractive enough for her to send the "approach me" smoke signals to. Don't, however, let the word "attractive" fool you. Attractive is not just about physical features—it is also about your nonverbal cues that let a woman know you are high status, a protector, a provider. In other words, the cues that let her know you are a Hero, rather than a Zero. But let's talk about physical features first.

All men worry about how they look. And here's the sad fact: Most men, as well as most women—regardless of how objectively attractive they are—think that they are *unattractive*. In one study men were asked whether they thought their penis size was above average, average, or below average. Most men said that their penis size was below average—a fact that is statistically impossible.

So, what physical features do women find most attractive in a man? The answer is symmetry. That's right, symmetry. Research shows that women are most drawn to the few men on the planet with symmetrical faces. So if the left and right sides of your face match up perfectly, you will most likely be a god among mere mortals, and women will be sending approach signals to you so quickly that you will need ninja-like skills to dodge them all. It turns out that roughly 53.5 percent of men have symmetrical faces, while roughly 58.5 percent of women have symmetrical faces.[1]

So, what about the rest—the symmetrically challenged?

Short of hiring a plastic surgeon, their best option is to show through body language that they are worthy of attention. Asymmetrical men have to send cues that will cause women to send their cues, which will then make the men think they have come up with the brave and brilliant idea of approaching these women.

It's an intricate dance, but all animals do it because of this small thing we like to call *evolution*. When you are at the grocery store buying your single-serving Hungry-Man dinner, you are probably *not* thinking about future shopping opportunities at Babies"R"Us; but all humans, including the women you are trying to attract, are biologically driven to try to reproduce with the person who will give them the most viable offspring. That's how the species survives, and that's how humans operate at the most basic and unconscious level. So, when you are in the frozen food aisle and a woman with a perfect hip-to-waist ratio walks by, it doesn't matter that your plan is to stay single until you are 60 years old and to never have children—you will still find your-self, for the 100th time that day, suddenly thinking about sex. You (and she) are biologically driven, and the only thing that gives you a chance in hell of actually having that woman notice you is send-ing out the cues that indicate you are good mating material. This woman (and every woman) is operating under extreme evolution-ary pressure to value certain qualities in a male. (Again, this is true whether the woman wants children or not.) Fail to send those cues and you can look forward to many, many nights spent eating Hungry-Man dinners alone.

Take Up Space

The first behavior that will make a woman pay attention is what scientists call "space maximizing." Think about it: The person who takes up the most space is considered the socially dominant person. This is true in the social systems of animals and in the social systems of humans. This is why the CEO of a company has a large corner office or why Jabba the Hutt was sprawled on a large throne with Princess Leia (and everyone else) below him.

Researchers Lee Ann Renninger, PhD, T. Joel Wade, PhD, and Karl Grammer, PhD, from the University of Vienna sought to determine the nonverbal cues that males give to increase the likelihood of females choosing them. After all, if it is the woman who initiates the approach from a man, how does she quickly and—without any background check whatsoever—choose which men to signal?

Their observational studies, published in *Evolution & Human Behavior,*[2] document the nonverbal behavior or body movements of males before they make contact with women. The men who "successfully made contact," meaning they didn't get slapped, shunned, or otherwise publicly rejected, had very different body language than the men who were unsuccessful in their approach.

The men who were successful were space maximizers, showing their dominance in the social setting by stretching out their legs, throwing an arm around their chair, or otherwise owning the space they occupied. The men who were successful also made "significantly more glancing behaviors." This means they looked a women in the eyes and often accompanied that with a smile. (Otherwise, staring a woman down is just creepy.) Successful men also made fewer "closed-body movements"—think of folding your arms across your chest like a schoolboy being scolded. If you are in a group of people and are practically hugging yourself, you are not going to be seen as socially dominant.[3] Never stand with one arm across your torso holding onto your other arm or crossing your legs at the knee—you might be comfortable, but from an evolutionary perspective, you can kiss your offspring goodbye.

Social dominance is also shown by what researchers call intragender touching. This amounts to something as simple as you slapping your buddy on the back or throwing an arm around his

STRESS IS NOT SEXY

According to research by Fhionna Moore, PhD, from the University of Dundee, women find low-stress men much more attractive than men with higher levels of cortisol (a stress hormone). Apparently remaining calm is another one of those evolutionary advantages that women are very attracted to. If there's a saber-toothed tiger attacking your cave, no woman wants a man who is going to freak out and end up fainting from all the excitement.[4]

shoulders, mano a mano. This signals social dominance and will make you more likely to get the go-ahead signal from a woman.

On the other end of the spectrum, research has also shown that if you are someone who fidgets or makes crazy, random nervous gestures with your hands, you're going to appear less confident, less socially dominant, and therefore less desirable to women. As we said in the beginning, women are attracted to confidence. Do you think the Dungeon Master could have displayed a nervous tic while making his decisions and still gotten the girl? Not a chance.

Now if this seems like a lot to remember, it will help you to think of the Clark Kent/Superman dichotomy. There is definite face symmetry shared by both, but Clark Kent was nervous; he stammered, fidgeted, fumbled, and did not get the girl. When he was Superman, he was confident, took up lots of space, and did not hesitate to go after the bad guys. His x-ray vision didn't hurt, either, when it came time to exhibit those glancing behaviors. When we say women are looking for a Hero, rather than a Zero, you can't go wrong if you model yourself after Superman.

You Know She's Interested When . . .

Sonja is a beautiful woman—we're talking supermodel level and up. But Sonja is often heard to complain that she rarely gets asked out on a date. Her girlfriends tell her that men are intimidated by her, but the truth is, Sonja is simply not giving out the signals that she is approachable. To men, she is an ice queen—not because of her regal beauty, but because she doesn't send out the nonverbal signals that indicate openness and approachability. Now, men might not consciously know that this is what's going on (until now), but to them Sonja appears to be standoffish, or even unfriendly. Whether or not men are interested in a woman is not strongly related to her objective attractiveness, but instead to the nonverbal signals she sends out.

Of course, men need to interpret the signals correctly.

Psychologist Monica Moore, PhD, of Webster University, observed over 200 women at singles bars, restaurants, parties, and other places. From her observations, she created a list of 52 things women do when they flirt. Women tilt their heads, give a particular man short glances, dart their eyes if he looks, run their fingers through their hair, lick their lips, and expose their necks. These women showed their palms to the man, hiked up their skirts a bit, revealed more of their legs, turned in their seats, or caressed an object, sometimes in suggestive, even sensual ways. They walked across the room, swaying their hips, and brushed by a man, touching him fleetingly with their thighs or breasts. Their actions were often subtle, but all were definite signals that a woman was interested and approachable. Many of these gestures are ones that women do unconsciously, not even knowing that they are doing them.

In short, when it comes to the intricate dance that men and women do when they are attracted to each other, meeting for the first time, and engaged in flirting, the women are in control—they are the choreographers. When Dr. Moore scored a woman's nonverbal behaviors, they predicted a man's approach to her with over 90 percent accuracy.

If she wants you, she will put a bid in your direction. The most common bid is direct eye contact. A smile. Repeatedly glancing at you and away from you. These are the signals; what you do with them is up to you.

A Word of Caution

Women will also let you know through nonverbal behaviors and cues when they're not interested. Now if you choose to approach without having gotten the signal, you are risking a high rejection percentage. Just as a woman will give clear signals when she wants you to approach, she will also give clear signals that are the equivalent of a No Trespassing sign.

If you approach a woman and she continues to talk to her friend, she's not interested. If she won't make eye contact with you while politely engaging in small talk or she is looking over your head and scanning the room, your chances are less than zero. If she yawns or leans or turns away, you need to move on. Now there are times when a woman is interested but may be particularly shy about making eye contact. In this case, she may show other signs of social anxiety, such as stuttering when she speaks to you or saying "ummm" a lot while speaking. But she will engage in conversation. Shy or not, if she's not interested, she will send you the cues to make that clear.

Where men go wrong is thinking that she will suddenly become interested once she finds out how fascinating, rich, or muscular they are. When she says no to a dance, a drink, or a conversation it does not mean that you should try harder. Rejection sucks, but no always means no. If you find a serious lack of interest from multiple women, day after day, or night after night, take another look at the cues you are sending. The point isn't to keep knocking on doors to find out who's attracted to you; the point is to make yourself as universally attractive as possible.

And attractive, as we've discussed earlier, has many, many components. Women find funny men more attractive, because humor is an indicator of intelligence. Women don't like meekness in a man, either, because meekness makes men seem less confident and less ambitious, and therefore weaker from an evolutionary perspective.

Remember to look into her eyes, smile, stand up straight (posture indicates confidence), and don't fidget. Channel your inner Hero, your inner Superman, and when all is said and done—if she's not interested, don't make it personal. If she doesn't want you, you don't want her. Mutual attraction is the only attraction worth having. Biology and experience draw you to certain people, and that's something you can only exert so much control over. We'll discuss this further in the next chapter.

As John's mother used to say, every pot has a lid, and all you can do is become the best, most attractive pot you can be. Your lid is waiting.

CHEAT SHEET *for* **HEROES**

Women are attracted to confidence and high status. Become the best "you" possible and exhibit the nonverbal behaviors that indicate social dominance, such as space maximization, male-to-male touching, relaxation, and looking into her eyes and smiling. Avoid fidgeting, poor posture, folding your arms across your chest, or crossing your legs at the knee.

Women control whether men approach them by exhibiting a series of nonverbal cues and indicators. Learn the signs that indicate she's interested.

★ She repeatedly glances at you and looks away.

★ She leans toward you while talking.

★ She points in your direction with her leg, foot, or shoulders.

★ She plays with or tosses her hair.

★ She fidgets with a piece of jewelry (like an earring) or strokes the stem of her glass.

YOU MIGHT BE A ZERO IF. . .

You ignore the signs that she is not attracted to you and pursue her anyway. Signals of disinterest include:

✖ She doesn't make eye contact (unless she's shy).

✖ She yawns repeatedly when you talk to her.

✖ She leans or turns her body away from you.

✖ She looks over your head or scans the room.

✖ She tells you she's not interested in you.

Additionally, you are not helping your cause if:

✖ You think hygiene and clothing don't matter.

✖ You think drunkenness is attractive.

✖ You don't make eye contact or smile at a woman you're interested in.

✖ Your posture or demeanor indicates weakness or you otherwise look like someone who can't keep her safe.

✖ You can't differentiate between confidence and arrogance. One is attractive to women; the other is not.

Chapter 4

FIRST IMPRESSIONS

Do's and Don'ts of Dating

I'm dating a woman now who,
evidently, is unaware of it.

—Garry Shandling

WHEN JOHN WAS 13 years old, he had his very first date. Her name was Linda. *Poor, poor, Linda.* John had no idea what a person did on a date. He thought about asking his parents, but who asks their parents for dating advice? He couldn't ask his cousin because she was only 5 at the time, and her idea of a date involved a tea party with stuffed animals. John decided to seek information at the only place he knew to seek information—the public library. He scoured the shelves for a book about dating. There were none.

He asked the reference librarian.

She asked him to leave.

Nearing panic, John went to the local bookstore and bought the first book he found that he thought *might* give him something, anything, to talk about on this date. It was a book of 10,000 jokes. He memorized about 300 of the jokes before his first date with Linda.

Then Aaron came along. Aaron was 3 months older than John and wise to the ways of women and dating. It was 1955, and Aaron was John's wingman long before the term had ever been invented.

Aaron told John the jokes were a good idea, but then he also told John that the one thing he needed to know was that "girls were real slow and stupid." He advised John to take Linda to a movie.

Then he told him exactly what to do. "Put your arm over the back of her chair and move it real, real slow. Girls don't notice this approach if it's very slow. Then slowly let your hand drop and grab onto her breast. She will love it, and you'll have the sex with her that night." Aaron always called it "the sex."

As soon as Linda opened her door, John started with, "Did you hear the one about the traveling salesman who asks the farmer if he can spend the night at his farm?" And he didn't stop during the entire walk to the movie theater. He regaled Linda with joke after joke, right up until they sat down in their seats in the theater.

The movie began, and John very suavely put his arm over the back of Linda's chair. Slowly, slowly, he inched his hand closer. He touched her shoulder. She didn't flinch or jump; she didn't seem to notice at all. Aaron had been right. Girls were stupid and John was going to have "the sex."

John felt his arm start to go a bit numb and tingly from the awkward reach around the back of the seat and the stretch down toward the breast, but still, millimeter by millimeter, he advanced until his hand was poised and ready to strike. And then his arm went completely numb, he lost all sensation, and his hand landed with an unceremonious thump right on top of Linda's breast.

This, she noticed. Linda gave John a dirty look, grabbed his arm, and flung it off her body with enough force that it knocked John completely off his chair. John lay on the floor of the movie theater and realized that sex was probably out of the question and this dating thing was too hard.

Climbing back into his chair, he did the only thing he really knew how to do. "Did you hear the one about the drunk who goes into a bar?"

Poor, poor, Linda.

Follow the Clues

We assume that if you are reading this book, you are past the age of 13, but you still may be just as confused about the world of dating. As you learned in the previous chapter, women control whether or not a man approaches her by giving nonverbal cues. You may think you are in the driver's seat, but the woman is the one who signals a green light for *go* or a red light for *stop right there, don't even attempt to drive that car in my direction.* Now, sometimes men get confused by the signals—what if it's a blinking red light, a yellow light, a flash of a green light? Could the signal be broken, did you miss it, should you drive forward anyway?

Here's a quick and easy test to check your signal reading ability. Let's say you are at a crowded club (or a coffee shop, or a concert, or the dog park). You see a woman look at you, smile, and then look away. She does this repeatedly. But then you start to wonder—could there be some Brad Pitt-looking guy right behind

"Your body language would suggest you're not having the best time on our first date."

you who is space maximizing up a storm and you don't even know it? Is she really looking at you? How can you be sure?

It's simple. Walk to the other side of the room. Or move to another table in the coffee shop. Or the far end of the dog park. Then see if she finds your eyes and starts the glance, smile, and look away routine all over again. Unless that Brad Pitt look-alike is creepily shadowing your every move, then you can be sure she is giving you the signal to approach.

Now it's important to remember that she is only signaling her interest in saying hello. Her first impression of you (without knowing anything about you) is strong enough that she'd like to know a little bit more. It's up to you to make your *next* first impression.

The First Conversation

We already discussed that the number one thing a woman is looking for in a man is trustworthiness, and that this means that you simply are who you say you are and you do what you say you are going to do. The goal of dating (if you are dating in hopes of finding the lid to your pot) is to find someone genuinely interested in you for who you really are, not who you are pretending to be while on a date. You don't have to be ready to find your one true lid. There's nothing wrong with dating a variety of lids. That is, after all, how you find out what lid is right for your pot. However, if your goal in dating is simply to have a lot of anonymous sex with anonymous women, there are probably other books that can tell you how to seduce women into bed under false pretenses. We have nothing against sex, casual or otherwise, as you will see in Chapter 9. But the premise of this book is that you are learning what every woman wants so that you can be the *you* that women will want most, not so you can pretend to be someone else just to score or deceive women.

If trustworthiness is about creating safety (physical and emotional), the way you create safety in a conversation is by being a good listener and being genuinely interested. John failed during his first date with Linda because he didn't show up as himself and because in all of his planning of the date he never once considered the date from Linda's point of view. You have to put the woman, rather than yourself, at the center of any encounter or date. John also didn't invite conversation. Instead he simply memorized what he was going to say. In 1955, jokes like John told were the equivalent of cheesy pickup lines—a means to an end that has nothing to do with the other person. Approaching a woman with a line rather than interest in getting to know her will get you nowhere fast. A woman may humor you a bit, but you are not being the man every woman wants. You are being another one of *those guys*. You know the ones we're talking about. The ones who approach a woman and say, "Baby, if you were words on a page, you'd be what they call fine print!"

Women are impressed with a guy who has emotional energy, who is passionate about whatever he's talking about, and who asks questions and really listens to the answers. In the Love Lab, we found that successful couples reported that their first impressions were positive and not superficial. It wasn't about how handsome or beautiful someone appeared to be, it was about interest, warmth, and a genuine desire to get to know the other person as a real person. Women are looking for transparency and honest conversation. If she asks you what you do for a living and you are vague, she won't feel safe. If you are talking to her and scanning the room (or scanning her breasts), she won't feel safe. If you ask her a question and then interrupt her answer, or you fail to ask a follow-up question related to her answer that shows you are really listening, guess what happens: She doesn't feel safe.

Women can be more tentative in conversation, especially first conversations, so put out the welcome mat of interest and invite her to talk about herself. Then make space for her to talk. Don't hurry her along and don't finish her sentences for her. In other words, don't dominate the conversation. Every woman has a story and your job is to invite her to tell that story. Ask her questions about her work, her life, and her interests, and keep it positive. If she starts thinking about negative things, she's going to associate those negative things with you.

Say, for example, you ask her what she does for a living and she answers that she's an attorney. What do you say next? A Zero will make a lawyer joke or say okay, and then ask her another question. A Hero will follow up with deeper questions: "What made you decide to go into law? What do you love about it?" Listen to her answers and ask follow-up questions. If she says she became a lawyer for her parents, and she hates the law, then you can ask her, "What would you rather be doing?" Ask her open-ended questions. Open-ended questions are answered with more than a word or two; they can't be answered with a simple yes or no. Their answers contain longer descriptions, explanations, or mental meanderings. They turn a finite question into an infinite answer. They are invitations. If the work questions seem like they are going nowhere or are not inspiring her to tell you about herself, you can ask another open-ended question: "What do you love to do when you are not working?" You can ask her where she's from or where she grew up—these are closed-ended questions—but then ask her what it was like to grow up there. What were high and low points about growing up there? Conversation is an art, and it's an art that puts *the other person* at center stage.

During this first conversation (and all future conversations), look into her eyes while she's speaking. A study by psychologists from Clark University had strangers gaze into each other's eyes for 2 minutes. This mutual eye gazing produced rapid and dramatically increased feelings of intimacy and affection among the strangers.[1] Now don't get all creepy about it. Remember to blink now and then—it's not a staring contest. There's a fine line between mutual gazing that inspires feelings of affection and relentless staring that makes her suddenly wonder if you're a serial killer.

CEOS WITH DEEP VOICES

Researchers at Duke University found that CEOs with lower voices manage bigger companies and, as a result, make more money. The research specifically found that a decrease in voice pitch of 22.1 hertz translates to an increase in company size of $440 million in assets. They also found that CEOs with lower-pitched voices earned an average of $187,000 a year more than CEOs with higher-pitched voices.[2]

Another point to consider during this first conversation is the tone of your voice. Professor David Feinberg, from the Department of Psychology, Neuroscience, and Behavior at McMaster University, is the director of the Voice Research Laboratory, and his studies over the last decade have shown that lower-pitched voices in men are considered more attractive to women, and also that men with deep voices have more children.[3] His research also looked at US presidential candidates between 1960 and 2000 and found that in all eight elections, the candidate with the lower voice won the popular vote.

So channel your inner James Earl Jones rather than your inner Mike Tyson when speaking to a woman. Try to speak at your fundamental frequency. To find your fundamental frequency, stand in the shower and use your thumb and index finger to lightly pinch the bridge of your nose. Now hum, varying the frequency. Your fundamental frequency causes the bones of your nose to vibrate the most. Actors use this pitch range to project in a theater without causing voice strain. Anxiety makes the pitch of your voice rise. Speaking naturally within your fundamental frequency, you are more likely to get her interest and get the date. And if you run for president someday, you're also more likely to get her vote. Be aware that this voice business is subtle. In other studies, it was a "breathy or tender" deep voice that got the girl, rather than an aggressive or intimidating deep-pitched voice.[4] As always, you want to attract her, not scare her.

The main point is that people like people who like them. If you like her, show her through words, actions, and your conversation and listening skills. Undivided attention is a powerful aphrodisiac.

You can also draw on the power of the unconscious mind. Famed social psychology researcher John Bargh, PhD, and his team at Yale University found that people naturally match each other's body language. (Think of a group of people all standing around in a circle, crossing their arms.) This is called "social glue." Subjects in their lab liked the researcher more and thought the interaction went better when the researcher had been mimicking the subjects' body postures and movements. People naturally take on each other's mannerisms and like each other as a result. You can use social glue on a date, as well. It happens automatically if you look at the woman—and pay attention. We're not suggesting you be overly contrived about this and don't want you to be flipping your hair back if she's flipping hers. Just pay attention to her words and her body language, and you'll start getting the social bonding going.

The next step is obvious: Ask for her phone number or ask her out on a date. And when you do ask, if it's appropriate, touch her forearm while you do it. Research shows greater compliance to a request if you have "light tactile contact."[5] So touch her forearm for 1 to 2 seconds while you are asking for a dance, or her number, or a date. It's another way of indicating your social status and confidence. Remember that it's a light touch—gentle and brief contact. Don't hold her arm in a death grip until she complies or come across as overly familiar. Brief. Playful. Confident.

All of this advice is given under the assumption that what you are seeking is a date and eventually a relationship—not "the sex." There's nothing wrong with wanting sex—everyone does. But the man every woman wants isn't a pickup artist or a hustler. He's real. He's a Hero, not a Zero. In the next chapter, we'll discuss how to make your move when it's time for seduction, but for now, all you are doing is seducing her into seeing you again.

There's a difference between men and women when it comes to sex with someone they've just met. Psychologists Russell D. Clark III, PhD, and Elaine Hatfield, PhD, conducted two experiments in which a male or female (of average attractiveness) approached an opposite-sex undergraduate and asked one of three questions.

1. Would you go out tonight?
2. Will you come over to my apartment?
3. Would you go to bed with me?

The great majority of males were willing to have a sexual liaison with a complete stranger, but not one woman answered yes to the third question.[6]

Psychologist Martin Voracek, PhD, in Austria, repeated the study and found that the female acceptance rate of women was not zero, but 6.1 percent.[7] Still, it's a relatively low figure compared to the men.

Of course, if you're like Lloyd in the movie *Dumb and Dumber,* you may be thinking 6 out of 100 is pretty good odds. "So you're telling me I have a chance," he would say.

We are not telling you to ask 100 women to go to bed with you, even if you live in Austria. We're telling you that women, for understandable evolutionary reasons, need to be more selective about their mates, so you'll need to pay attention and build trust during every stage of the courtship dance.

The First Date

The nonverbal mating cues have been sent, the first conversation went well, and you've asked her out on a date—now what? Dating is another way to demonstrate your Hero status. It's not about how much you spend; it's about putting her front and center. You can plan a special date that doesn't cost a lot of money—a picnic, a hike, a trip to a free museum or cultural event. Be creative. Be playful. Plan an adventure.

We'll let you in on a little secret. Riding a roller coaster, bungee jumping, or doing something else adventurous with a little bit of fear mixed in can be helpful on your date. The physiological response to fear is quite similar to the physiological response to arousal. The right amygdala—the part of the brain where you most experience fear—is also one part of the brain where you experience sexual arousal. The two can often get confused. Hormones also play a powerful role. When you engage in an activity that is new, exciting, or dangerous, the same hormonal brew (dopamine, norepinephrine, and phenylethylamine) gets released as when you fall in love. So do something exciting and adventurous together on your date—arouse your central nervous systems and arouse each other.

Dating is also about continuing the conversation and getting to know each other. Ask her about her interests, her passions, her life dreams, her bucket list. Find out where she's traveled and what she loves to do. Ask her who her best friends are, and find out what they are like and what she loves about them. Ask about her family or pets (if she has any). Ask her where she went to school, and supply open-ended questions about what learning she

did that most caught her attention and imagination. Now there's a fine line between interrogation and conversation, so be sure to really listen, rather than have it seem like you are checking off a list of questions like it's a job interview. Body language is still important. Hygiene is also important. Being a gentleman is most important. Open doors, walk on the busy side of the sidewalk, walk in stride with her, demonstrate your protective instincts. Ask yourself how a Hero would act and you're more likely to get another date.

So be protective, be a gentleman, and also—this is most important—be fully you. Be prepared to share your own passions, your own interests, and your own life dreams. But listen first. Talk about your best friends, tell her what they're like, and talk about where you have traveled and what you loved and hated about traveling. Unlike men, women are much more geared for collaboration, not competition, so if you are discussing something and you have opposing viewpoints, don't tell her she is wrong. You can say, "That's interesting. Tell me more." After listening and responding with interest, it's okay to say, "Okay, here's my viewpoint," but don't present your differences in a way that devalues her.

Don't talk about ex-girlfriends. Don't tell stories that turn you into a victim. Talk about who you are and what you think about where you are going in life.

Don't make the fatal mistake some men make: Don't ask her how she thinks the date is going. Don't ask her if she likes you. You will come off as needy and insecure. Tune in to her, and you will already know the answers to these questions. Insecurity is an attraction killer every time, and nothing will drop you into the friend zone faster.

Assuming you've stayed out of the friend zone, you'll want to read the next chapter, where we will discuss the science of seduction and how to make your move.

CHEAT SHEET
for **HEROES**

- ★ Ask open-ended questions.
- ★ Be authentic, but try to speak in your lowest register if your natural voice sounds a bit like Mickey Mouse on helium.
- ★ Create safety in conversations by being a good listener.
- ★ Put the woman at the center of any conversation or date.
- ★ Look into her eyes and match her gestures in a natural and easy way.
- ★ Briefly touch her forearm when you ask her to dance, ask for her number, or ask her on a date.
- ★ Be creative when planning your first date. Think of something adventurous, playful, or exciting to do.
- ★ Be a gentleman—open doors, pull out her chair.
- ★ Be protective and confident.

YOU MIGHT BE A ZERO IF. . .

- ✖ You use cheesy pickup lines.
- ✖ You make overt sexual innuendoes.
- ✖ You dominate the conversation, interrupt her, or only talk about yourself.
- ✖ You don't ask questions that will help you get to know her and help her tell her story.
- ✖ You think spending a lot of money on a date means you will get laid.
- ✖ You don't plan a date that makes her feel special and important.
- ✖ You stare at her breasts while she is talking or scan the room checking out other girls when you are with her.

THE MAN'S GUIDE

PART THREE

TO WOMEN

Romancing a Woman

Chapter 5

MAKING YOUR MOVE

The Science of Seduction

THERE'S A MEN'S aftershave that advertises itself as "the most powerful known to mankind." The company promises that once you douse yourself in this cologne, it will attract a woman and make her mysteriously drawn to you. She will listen intently to your every word and be overcome by a desire to touch you. If you pay her a compliment, she will swoon. Wearing it will "subconsciously put her mind at ease," and it will assist you in seduction.

What is in this magic scent that will virtually hypnotize a woman? Pheromones. Male pheromones, to be exact. We can't attest to the power of pheromones in a bottle, but naturally occurring pheromones are chemical signals released from the skin and sweat glands of both animals and humans. And they're powerful. They are what make some people just "smell right" to others, and they can put a woman at ease and cause her to feel an attraction to you. That's the good news. The bad news is that for every individual, there's a percentage of people who are drawn to their pheromones and a percentage who are not. There's nothing you can do about this—it's chemistry.

Notice that we said pheromones are going to make a woman feel an attraction to you, not tear off her clothes in a fit of uncontrollable lust that makes her want to climb you like a tree. No matter what any company advertisement says, human pheromones are more about attraction and sensuality than sexual compulsion. Now if you were a wild boar, it would be a different story. Female boars are driven crazy by androstenone and androstenol, two male sex pheromones present in the saliva of the male. If she's fertile, she will go at him like, well, a wild boar.

Wild boars have all the luck.

A woman's sense of smell is stronger than a man's (estrogen is the culprit), and that's why women can detect odors far more acutely than men do. The man every woman wants doesn't smell like a wet dog locked inside a gym locker next to a pair of old socks. Your smell matters. Some of how you smell is under your control. Showers. Deodorant. Clean socks. They matter. But you can't control your pheromones. They are what they are, and they affect the brain and the nervous system of a woman through vomeronasal receptors at the base of the nasal cavity. These receptors detect pheromones subconsciously, and a woman will react to the scent both physically and emotionally. Have you ever noticed a woman smelling the top of a baby's head? A baby's head emits pheromones that cause the female brain to produce oxytocin—the hormone responsible for feelings of love and intimacy and pleasure. Forget male sex hormones in a bottle—the company that can bottle the scent of a baby's head might possess the ultimate secret weapon in attracting a woman.

Pheromones are powerful biology, driving us toward those who are the best genetic fit for reproduction. That's why a girl will think her brother smells awful, while he may smell great to his girlfriend. Pheromones are a two-way street, and just as you will smell good to some women and not to others, some women will just smell right to you and some won't. It's not personal; it's biology.

In 2005, scientists at Karolinska Institute, a medical university in Stockholm, exposed straight men, gay men, and straight women to chemicals found in male and female sex hormones. One was a testosterone derivative found in men's sweat and the other was an estrogen derivative found in women's urine. Using brain imaging, the research found that the chemical in men's sweat lit up the hypothalamus in both the women and the homosexual men. (The hypothalamus is the area of the brain responsible for reproductive behavior.) The chemical from women's urine lit up the hypothalamus only in the heterosexual men.[1]

Scientists at the Monell Chemical Senses Center in Philadelphia collected the natural body odors of both straight and gay men and women. (Don't ask how they did this. You really don't want to know.) Their study achieved similar results, finding that gay men preferred the odor of other gay men, while straight men preferred the odor of women. The women in the study also chose the odor of straight men over gay men.[2] More proof that your sense of smell is a powerful reproductive tool.

You can peruse all the online dating sites you want, looking for the perfect woman, but what those sites can't perfectly match up is how you are going to smell to your date and how she is going to smell to you. "Pheromone parties" began in 2010 when Judith Prays, an artist from New York City who wondered why she was so attracted to the scent of some men and not others, decided to test what it would be like if people only chose each other based on smell. She had 40 singles sleep in a shirt for 3 nights and then bring the shirt to the party in a plastic bag. She numbered each of the bags and divided them up by gender. During the party, people smelled the numbered bags and chose people whose scent they were most attracted to. The results? Twelve couples "hooked up" and a full 50 percent of those went on to have long-term relationships. Since that time, pheromone parties have become popular in major cities around the world.

The science of attraction isn't just limited to the olfactory senses, however. There's another interesting field to explore called philematology—the science of kissing.

The First Kiss

Now, we don't want to freak you out or add any dating pressure, but the truth is, a woman always, always remembers the first kiss. Clumsy or passionate. Tender or aggressive. Juicy or dry. Foreheads or noses knocking. Who turned their face to the right, who turned to the left. Sounds and smells. A woman remembers it all. And the first kiss matters.

It matters a lot.

John Bohannon, PhD, a psychologist from Butler University, surveyed 500 people to compare memories of significant life experiences (including losing their virginity), and the first kiss beat out everything else on the list. It was the "most vivid memory in the minds of those being surveyed." He reports that people could recall 90 percent of the details, no matter how long ago it took place.[3] To add even a little more pressure, evolutionary psychologist Gordon Gallup, PhD, of the University at Albany reports that 66 percent of women say they have ended a relationship because of a kiss that did not go well.[4] So what is so important about a kiss?

Look at it this way: Your lips have a huge number of nerve endings and a bigger-than-expected representation in the sensory cortex of your brain. And the right kiss can stimulate these nerve endings and release a flood of feel-good hormones in a woman's brain. Ignite those nerve endings, and she's going to feel like she just drank a glass of very expensive champagne. Fail to ignite them, and you might as well kiss her goodbye. Chemistry is everything when it comes to kissing, and like with pheromones, you'll either be a match or you won't. There are ways, however, to increase the odds that your first kiss will ignite a spark.

www.cartoonstock.com

ORAL HYGIENE. If you just ate a can of sardines followed up by some roasted garlic with Brie cheese, rethink moving in for that kiss. Remember that a woman's sense of smell is acute, and you reeking of something foul smelling is *not* cute.

BE CONFIDENT. Did Rhett Butler hesitate when he kissed Scarlett O'Hara in *Gone with the Wind*? No. He told her she "should be kissed often and by someone who knows how." Then he proved he was the man for the job. There's a reason the covers of so many romance novels show a woman in the midst of a passionate kiss. Nothing is more of a mood killer than a man who asks for permission. "May I kiss you now?" It's polite, but it's not likely to ignite any chemical cocktails in her brain. Instead, read her nonverbal signals to know if it's the right moment.

READ THE SIGNALS. You can tell if a woman wants you to kiss her. When she's interested, she will give most of her attention to your eyes and lips. She may lick her own lips or bite down on her bottom lip. Look into her eyes. Look at her lips. See if she's smiling. She may not go for the kiss herself (no romance novel cover has the woman bending the man backward to kiss him), but she will send the signal when she wants you to go for it.

GO SLOW. Don't dive at her face like she's a slice of pizza and you're starving. Remember, research shows she's going to remember every detail of this first kiss (or at least 90 percent of it) for a very long time. You don't want her to remember you lunging at her like a rabid dog. Move your face a bit closer to hers and see if she moves back or stays where she is. If she leans away, you may be reading the signals wrong. If she stays where she is or moves in a little closer herself, then it's time.

BUILD ANTICIPATION. Touch her face. Stroke her hair. Move your lips closer to hers and let them hover a bit so she feels your breath on hers (see Oral Hygiene on page 65). Let the attraction build and let the desire to touch lips build. You want her to want you to kiss her. Anticipation that something wonderful is about to happen releases dopamine and makes the actual experience even more pleasurable. Your ultimate goal is to make her want to kiss you more than she wants to breathe.

KISS THE GIRL. Touch your lips slowly to hers and simply pause. Feel the sensations. Be in the moment. Don't dive right in and cram your tongue into her mouth. It's a kiss, not an assault. Increase the pressure and respond as she responds. If she opens her mouth, then gently touch tongues. Men's saliva contains testosterone, and testosterone increases sex drive in a woman. This doesn't mean you should attempt to get as much of your saliva into her mouth as possible; that will not increase her sex drive. Also, do not assume that smearing saliva around outside her mouth is a good idea. A little wet inside the mouth is fine—kissing her like a Saint Bernard is not. Keep it clean. Drool is not sexy.

TRUST YOUR INSTINCTS. Kissing is a dance, and every dance between two people is unique. She's going to follow your lead, and then you should follow hers. If she pulls back, then end the kiss. If your instincts tell you that her nerve endings are igniting, then keep on kissing her. Long kisses are wonderful.

TOUCH HER. A kiss happens with the lips, but the hands and arms enhance it. Stroke her face or her hair. Put your arms around her. Cup the back of her neck. Do anything with your hands but leave them resting limply at your sides. Making her feel safe in your arms will make her want to be there more often. The first kiss is probably *not* the time to go for her breasts.

So now your pheromones are in alignment and your first kiss made her see rainbows and dancing unicorns. What now? In the movies (depending on the rating), this is where the screen will either fade to black or you will both rip off your clothes and make mad, passionate love that would make even wild boars blush.

We can't tell you what to do next. Well, we can. And we will. But before we get to *that* chapter, we're going to put the brakes on. Whether this first kiss leads to a hookup or a relationship is up to the two of you, but before we discuss how to be a great lover, we're going to help you figure out whether a woman has potential for long-term monogamy or serious dating. It's hard to make rational decisions when you are flooded with oxytocin and perhaps not using the organ most suited for long-term thinking. Therefore, you should keep your wits about you. Your kissing may have made her absolutely crazy, or she may actually be absolutely crazy. In the next chapter, we'll help you spot the difference.

CHEAT SHEET for HEROES

★ Pheromones are chemical signals that lead to attraction and a sense of well-being when you are with someone who just "smells right."

★ A woman's sense of smell is much more acute than a man's, and your pheromones will smell right to some women and not to others. It's not personal.

★ You do have control over your non-pheromone-related smell. Practice good hygiene accordingly.

★ A bad first kiss is a relationship killer.

★ A woman will remember a first kiss more than she will remember losing her virginity and other big life moments. Make that kiss one worth remembering.

★ Kissing releases a flood of feel-good hormones.

★ You can learn to give a great first kiss.

YOU MIGHT BE A ZERO IF. . .

✖ You disregard your personal hygiene and believe that every woman should love your musky scent.

✖ You ignore the signs that she's either attracted to you or not. (Meaning you fail to make your move or you make your move too soon.)

✖ You treat a first kiss like it's a means to an end, rather than an important and memorable experience.

✖ You don't build anticipation for a kiss and move in too fast.

✖ You ram your tongue down her throat and assault her with saliva-filled sloppiness.

✖ You disregard the importance of tender touch during a kiss.

✖ You don't make her feel safe in your arms.

Chapter 6

IS SHE MORE THAN A HOOKUP?

Reading a Woman's True Profile

YOU'VE SEEN EACH other across a crowded room, felt the spark of attraction, pheromone has met pheromone, and your brain chemistry has started bubbling. You've gotten close to each other and she looks right, smells right, feels right. You're dating, or you're hooking up, and it's the morning (week, month) after, and while both parties have been on their best behavior, the question remains—is she more than a hookup?

It's a great question, but to give it real consideration, it's best not to decide while you are tangled in the bedsheets—with oxytocin, testosterone, and dopamine surging. Oxytocin, the hormone of bonding and attachment, is released during orgasm (which is why that "friends with benefits" thing never seems to work out the way people plan), and it impairs your ability to make sound decisions. Even affection of the nonorgasmic kind can send oxytocin surging. Oxytocin makes you feel great, but it not only clouds your judgment—it can shut down the fear response in your brain.

To evaluate the impact of oxytocin on decision making, researchers at the University of Zurich in Switzerland had participants play a trust game involving money.[1] The test subjects were given money and told they could keep the money or share it with another person. If they shared the money, the dollar amount tripled. This wasn't, however, an experiment in investing, it was an experiment in trust and sound decision making. You see, the person they "invested" the money with also had a choice—whether to keep all of the money and violate the trust of the investor or to repay the trust and give some of the money back.

During the game, both sets of investors were told that the other person kept all of the money. Participants in the study who had been given the placebo decreased how much money they were willing to trust the other person with after learning of the betrayal. Those who received a nasal spray of oxytocin, however, continued to share their money with the other person. The fact that they had been duped did not change their behavior at all.

And in case you're thinking that the group who had gotten the oxytocin must just be stupid about money, think again. During this game, scientists were monitoring the brains of the participants, and the group that had inhaled the oxytocin showed a decrease in activity in the part of the brain that is responsible for fear—the amygdala.

Oxytocin has the power to cause bad decision making that can harm not only your wallet, but also your heart. When you're in the first stages of attraction (love, lust, or whatever you want to call it), you're experiencing a cascade of hormones that induce a state that psychologists called *limerence*. You may not know the word, but you know the feeling. It's falling in love, it's what makes you think about the woman all the time. It's what makes you able to go without sleep and without food. It induces feelings of euphoria and ecstasy. It makes life more erotic and thrilling and beautiful.

It also makes you ignore a lot of warning signs. Put it this way: If Michael Douglas's character, Dan, had stopped for a moment and been aware that he was in limerence and drowning in a hormonal cocktail in the film *Fatal Attraction,* he might never have had an affair with Glenn Close's character, Alex, and she might never have boiled that bunny on his stove top.

Limerence can also make you believe that you are actually thinking logically when you're not. So when you are deciding if she's more than a hookup, make sure it's you in control of your thinking and not just the oxytocin receptors getting flooded in your amygdala, making you fearless. And if you find your brain starting to make excuses for some not-so-great behavior on the part of your object of affection, we'll let you in on another little secret: People don't change. That's right. At their core, who they are and how they treat others will not change. This is true for men and for women. So pay attention to the red flags popping up around her— you know, the ones you're ignoring because you're in limerence.

It wasn't hot, extramarital monkey sex that turned Alex into a bunny killer; she was a bunny killer from the start. Dan just chose to ignore the signs.

Obviously, Alex had a larger personality disorder, and we'll discuss some of those later in the chapter. But first let's discuss another possible reason, other than your hormones, that you might be drawn to one particular woman or another.

Imprinting

Research shows that whether or not people experienced close and loving relationships with their parents or caregivers early in life has a profound influence on their relationships later in life. Even if you have no memory of your early childhood experiences, they can affect how you feel and behave in your romantic life later on. A 20-year study showed that infants who had close and loving relationships with their caregivers during the first 18 months of life (these infants were called "securely attached" by the researchers) were better at handling conflict in their adult relationships. Infants who weren't securely attached during this critical time showed more difficulty in romantic relationships and were less committed to their relationships as adults.[2]

So does this mean you should only get involved with women who had close and loving caregivers from birth to toddlerhood? Of course not. If perfect early caregivers were the criteria for a relationship, the population would die out. None of us had perfect parents. But it is good to look at how these early imprints can affect both how you are in a relationship and how your partner is in a relationship.

Your early childhood experiences can also affect whom you choose as a partner. Even infants already show a preference for faces that look like their caregivers. Sometimes your choice of a mate will end up being someone who has the character traits of your primary caregiver. For better or worse, your brain is trying to re-create those very first imprints.

In the early 1900s, Konrad Lorenz became the first scientist to study imprinting. He was a naturalist who discovered that when young ducklings and goslings hatched, they would become attached to the first moving object they saw. Now normally this would be their mother, but Lorenz was able to get the birds to attach to him and even to inanimate objects like rain boots and an electric train. These birds formed a bond with whatever was in front of them during the critical period after their birth. Lorenz became their parent, and once they were attached, they couldn't be dissuaded. Much to Lorenz's surprise, when these ducks and geese grew up they would court and try to mate with humans, including Lorenz, rather than with other ducks and geese.

Of course no man wants to think he is attracted to the hot woman in the grocery store because she reminds him of his mother. That's a romance killer. But the forces that draw men and women to each other can be a complex and fascinating mix of nature and nurture, and it never hurts to keep your eyes and mind wide open when you find yourself irresistibly drawn to someone. And it also never hurts to do this *before* the two of you start having orgasms together.

Whether you've already crossed that bridge or not, it's important to pause and ask yourself some key questions before you take the relationship any further. This is how you can discover her true profile.

Her True Profile

Watch how your romantic partner treats her pets, friends, and family, and you'll get a good idea about how she will treat you in a relationship. Step back and try to observe her as objectively as you can. Is she kind? Is she respectful? Is she patient? Does she show compassion, is she considerate, or is she self-centered? Knowing her true profile means knowing her heart and mind, as well as her body. Do you trust her? Do you feel a sense of ease in interactions with her? Can you laugh together easily? Do you get her sense of humor? Does she get yours? If you do not know her well enough to answer these questions, or if you do not understand her well, your future relationship with her could get complicated—really complicated.

HEART. Try to notice if she is kind or if she complains about her friends and family all of the time. If something negative happens, does she blame others? Does she take any responsibility for miscommunications with friends and family? Is she honest in her other relationships, or does she lie and make excuses? Is she loyal? Does she keep the secrets entrusted to her, or do you hear her gossiping shortly after a friend or family member confides in her? Remember, people don't really change their basic character, and if she doesn't value trust and loyalty with those closest to her, she won't value it with you. Is she open-minded, or closed? Is she conscientious (she keeps promises and does what she commits to)? Is she agreeable, or does she provoke others and stoke conflict and disagreement? Is she "neurotic"? The technical term "neurotic" really means two possible cognitive styles: (1) she sees potential negativity everywhere, so she approaches any new situation with an expectation of total disaster, and/or (2) she ruminates endlessly on every small negative event.

MIND. Do her words and actions match up? Does she follow through with what she says she is going to do? Is she trusting or suspicious of you? Does she say she trusts you but looks through your phone or interrogates you about where you've been? Is she accepting of your friends, or does she find some fault with every one of them? Does she snoop through your drawers, want to read your e-mail, or question you about the women who are part of your social media network? Does she text you repeatedly without waiting for a reply? Assuming you are not engaging in player-like behavior and giving her reason for suspicion, all of these are red flags. Pay attention.

BODY. Is there sexual chemistry and attraction? Yes, it might be fun to have a good intellectual debate and some witty banter, but if there's no attraction between you, it's not likely to magically appear 200 intellectual debates down the road. Here's the thing about that limerence we mentioned earlier—it's highly selective. Not everyone will set off your cascade of feel-good hormones, and you won't send every girl you meet into a hormonal brain fog. If it doesn't happen in the beginning of a relationship, it's not going to happen later. Save yourself the time and energy—biology is a powerful thing that does not respond to manipulation. You can fake it for a while. She can fake it for a while. But you know when there is attraction and when there's not. Friends with benefits might get you through some lonely nights, but it's not going to satisfy you or her unless you are wildly attracted to each other. A great relationship is a mix of heart, mind, and body, and only a Zero settles for less than all three.

Those are some of the questions to ask yourself while your brain is not in danger of an oxytocin overdose. There are some personality types—and personality disorders—that will cause an enormous amount of grief in your life. You know the expression, "Don't put your ____ in crazy." This is a Mad Lib for your love life. Fill in the blank with whatever body part applies. We once saw a list of suggestions for a happy life. Number one was, "Choose your partner carefully. Your relationship will cause you 90 percent of the joy or sorrow in your life." This is not an exaggeration. Be on the lookout for and stay clear of the following characters.

THE DAMSEL IN DISTRESS. Does she present herself as a victim? Does she endlessly talk about the negative relationships in her life? Friends who have betrayed her? Past boyfriends who have cheated on her or let her down in some way? Does she tend to divide people into two categories, the Good and the Bad? Be careful. You may at first be the One True Good Guy, or the Rescuer, but eventually you will probably join the list of Bad Guys. Does she dwell on her physical ailments, personal traumas, or family woes? Now, in the course of dating and getting to know each other, you will share your personal histories, and most personal histories do include some painful things. But the question is, does she derive her identity from her trauma? Does she seem to relish the role of being a victim, or does she talk about what she's learned from past mistakes, heartaches, or traumas? There's a big difference between the two. If she feels that everyone in her life has let her down, then you could be the next name on that list.

THE PRINCESS. Does she present herself as if she's above everyone else? Does she treat others badly—waiters, service workers, strangers—and act as if they are beneath her in class, status, or value? If so, you may have a princess on your hands. Princesses rarely say "thank you" when you open a door or pull out a chair for them. They swirl about in a cloud of entitlement and often demand you spend a lot of money to show you care. A Princess will often have unrealistic expectations of you. You may be her prince at first, but ultimately you'll find yourself in the ranks of all her other lowly subjects. She lacks empathy and common courtesy, and she will put others down to feel better about herself. There was once a *New Yorker* cartoon of a Princess who angrily said to a waiter, "Do you know who I think I am?"

THE COMPETER. Does she lead with her success? Are the first words out of her mouth always about her conquests or achievements, and does she rarely show interest in you? Does she try to one-up you or other people around her? The Competer is, obviously, competitive, and she often has a chip on her shoulder. She will flirt with other people to make you jealous just so you know how lucky you are to be with her. This character type delights in other people's mistakes. She is controlling of others and also of herself. She may be perfectionistic. This is the kind of woman who may have very restricted eating behaviors and who may struggle to experience joy and pleasure. The Competer is no fun to be around.

THE DRAMA QUEEN. Do drama and chaos seem to follow her around? Is life a series of her problems, one after another, and she looks to you to fix them all? Is every day a new crisis? Now most people want a partner, not a project, but some men find themselves drawn into the swirling chaos that surrounds the Drama Queen. She runs out of gas, gets locked out of her house, and has endless drama with exes and friends alike. She may also have a drug or alcohol problem. Does she have more than two or three drinks in an evening? Are her pupils overly large or overly small, which are signs of potential drug use? Does she refuse to eat? Can she have a good time if it doesn't involve drinking or partying? The Drama Queen is a lot of work, and ultimately a person is not a fixer-upper. Are you willing to accept her just as she is if nothing changes?

This character list is by no means an exhaustive study of the types of women to avoid when asking yourself if she's more than a hookup, but rather some general guidelines to go by. There are some traits that are indicative of a larger personality disorder, and there can be a fine line between being a Damsel in Distress and having a diagnosis of borderline personality disorder; or being a Princess and having a clinical diagnosis of narcissistic personality disorder; or between being a Drama Queen and having a serious substance abuse problem.

The most important question to ask yourself about the woman you want to date or have a relationship with is this: How does she make you feel when you are with her? Is there a sense of ease in relating and laughing that makes you feel like you've somehow come home? Do you feel energized and happy? Are you able to talk endlessly and communicate well? Do you have the same values? Do you want to know everything about her and bring her to meet your friends and family? Does she make you feel good about yourself? Does she bring out your inner Hero?

If your body, mind, and heart are all in alignment with hers, then there's a very good chance she's more than a hookup.

★ Oxytocin can cloud your judgment and lower your fear response. It is the bonding hormone that gets released during orgasm and from affection. That's why platonic sex is an oxymoron.

★ Limerence is that first stage of attraction or love during which you obsessively think about the other person, can't sleep, feel highly sensual, and are high on love. The cascade of hormones flooding your body during limerence can cause you to ignore the warning signs or red flags in any potential relationship.

★ You can be attracted to someone because of your hormones or because of imprinting from your first 18 months. Ask yourself why you might be drawn to a particular woman, and stay aware of your conscious and unconscious motivations.

★ A woman is more than a hookup if you feel a connection in body, mind, and heart.

★ If there's no physical connection or chemistry at first, there never will be.

YOU MIGHT BE A ZERO IF. . .

✖ You ignore the warning signs and disregard the red flags in a potential relationship.

✖ You settle for a Damsel in Distress, a Princess, a Competer, or a Drama Queen.

✖ You make relationship decisions based on physical attraction alone.

✖ You let a woman make you feel bad about yourself, or you put up with rude or difficult behavior.

✖ You believe you can have sex and not get attached.

✖ You think you can "fix" her.

THE MAN'S GUIDE

PART FOUR

TO WOMEN

Making Love
to a Woman

Chapter 7

IMAGE IS EVERYTHING

Understanding How Women View Their Bodies

Be not ashamed women . . . You are the gates of the body, and you are the gates of the soul.

—Walt Whitman

No one ever told me I was pretty when I was a little girl. All little girls should be told they're pretty, even if they aren't.

—Marilyn Monroe

WE CAN PROVIDE a blueprint that details the anatomy of a woman's body. We can diagram it and tell you what buttons to push and which nerve endings to ignite. We will give you this guide in the next chapter, but before we navigate the sensual and sexual landscape of a woman's body, we need to explore the female form through a slightly different lens. In order to truly understand a woman's body, you have to first understand a woman's relationship with her body. And the truth is, this relationship is far more complex than can be expressed in any anatomical diagram.

Men adore the female body. It's soft. It's smooth. It has endless curves to roam your hands up and down. Let's be perfectly honest: Men crave a woman's body and never get tired of looking at a woman's body. And when that body belongs to your woman, you let her know how much you love her body, over and over again.

If you don't, you should.

A Hero lets a woman know through small comments just how great she looks in that color dress or how amazing her shoulder looks with the light hitting it just that way. Heroes tell a woman how beautiful her face looks in the moonlight and how gorgeous her smile is. A Hero will tell a woman how stunning she looks nursing the baby or how pretty she is first thing in the morning, with sleep still in her eyes and a face free of makeup. A Hero tells a woman how wonderful it feels to make love to her and shows her just how much he loves every part of her.

Men hope that these moments of spontaneous appreciation of her body will sink in. They hope that these words and the responses to her that are beyond words will filter through all the layers of self-doubt that society has imposed on her. They hope that the way they touch her and appreciate her every curve will sink in. They hope to reverse all the unfair and nasty comments others have made about her body, as well as those she has made about herself when she looked in the mirror on a bad day.

This is no small task.

Women view between 400 and 600 advertisements a day, and one out of every 11 of these ads has a direct message about what ideal feminine beauty is *supposed* to look like. By the time a woman is 60, she will have viewed about 6 million of these messages telling her what a woman's appearance *should* be. And guess what? It's virtually impossible to live up to this digitally manipulated and unreal standard of beauty. Over the last 2 decades, many of these idealized images of women have been airbrushed or photoshopped and so have grown even more unrealistic and unattainable. Even the models themselves don't look anything like they're portrayed. Many research studies have proven the negative impact of this flood of images of the idealized female body. The end result is that most women have a painful relationship with the image they see in the mirror.

Humor columnist Dave Barry says that the only appropriate response to a woman asking you, "Do I look fat in this?" is to fall to the floor and pretend you're having a heart attack. Now all men have gotten that question, but you can't go around faking heart attacks year after year. The real response to this question—the Hero's response to this question—is this: "You are beautiful no matter what you wear." That's it. There is no other answer. Ever. This should be a law, because there are definite fines and penalties if you don't answer exactly this way. Trust us on this one.

"DO YOU PROMISE TO TELL THE TRUTH, THE WHOLE TRUTH, AND NOTHING BUT THE TRUTH, EXCEPT IF YOUR WIFE ASKS IF SHE LOOKS FAT?"

Most women have been taught from an early age that their physical attractiveness is their greatest asset and their most intrinsic way of pleasing others and getting love. A woman doesn't see herself separately from her body, and therefore she often defines her worth in terms of her body. Beauty for women is a survival strategy, and there is constant pressure to be beautiful and to compare what she sees in the mirror to what society tells her is beautiful. Men and women alike have all been brainwashed by the standards of beauty defined by society at large and supported by the fashion and entertainment industries. You can tell her she's beautiful all day long, but if a woman feels that her body deviates from the standard image of beauty, then she is going to feel that her body is ugly. If she feels like her body is ugly, she's not going to feel good about herself as a person. If she doesn't feel good about herself, she's going to have a hard time enjoying her body—or enjoying *you* enjoying her body. It's a vicious cycle.

And the problem is, a woman doesn't feel that she can "build" her beauty like she can her physical strength, her stamina, her knowledge, her competence, or her wisdom. She doesn't feel that she can build her attractiveness the way she can her résumé. In fact, media messages tell her that her beauty will only deteriorate as she ages. Men are measured by their prowess, success, performance, and ability to be effective in their chosen field or occupation. Women are not only judged on all of those qualities, but also how they look and dress in the process. While men pretty much have a uniform for success—suit, tie, shoes, good haircut if you're really trying hard—women are scrutinized for a million little choices. What signal will it send to wear pants instead of a skirt? Are these colors too bright? Is this jewelry appropriate for this activity, and if so, how expensive does it look? Is this makeup going to send the wrong message? How polished is this hairstyle? When women take forever to get out the door, it's not vanity—it's

because she is constantly reminded that people will treat her differently based on how she looks. It's not right or fair, but that's what women are up against.

And as a man, you might think it's funny to comment on the doughnut she's eating or the size of her thighs—but it's not. And for every disparaging thing you say, you're going to need to say hundreds if not thousands of complimentary things to make up for it. Nothing cuts deeper for a woman than criticism of the way she looks. The man every woman wants never does this.

What you can do is try to understand what it's like to have a chronic and painful preoccupation with appearance and to feel like you are always coming up short. You can try to understand the tremendous need for social approval that causes women to constantly diet, shop for new clothing, overexercise, check their looks in the mirror, and consider plastic surgery a "solution" to the normal process of aging. A woman's self-esteem is heavily dependent on her own appraisal of her body. A bad moment on the scale can send her into an emotional tailspin. There are very good and deep reasons why her relationship with her own body is fragile. And you can understand that if she feels ugly, it is difficult for her to accept your appreciation of her body.

Of course, you can't reverse all the negative things she's heard or felt throughout her lifetime, but a little understanding goes a long way. You can't single-handedly fight a societally imposed impossible standard of beauty—not even the most heroic of men can do that—but you can help her feel beautiful in the mirror of your eyes.

She will feel beautiful if you only have eyes for her when you are with her. She will feel beautiful if you show her she's beautiful by loving every part of her with your eyes, your hands, and your lips.

Let's face it, women think men are measuring and comparing them in the same way they measure and compare themselves. Your job is to make sure that, clothed or naked, she knows how attractive and beautiful she is to you. As we said in the beginning of this book, men can make or break any relationship, and they can also make or break any relationship a woman has with her body. You can't control the fashion industry, but you can try to see how you, as well as the women in your life, are being brainwashed, and you can start to see your partner with the loving eyes of an artist, appreciating each of her unique qualities and curves. Despite what Madison Avenue says, being thin is not everything. Men want women to be healthy, to be curvy, to be, well, women.

Clinical psychologist and author Joni Johnston, PsyD, writes that after the bubonic plague in Europe wiped out one-third of the population, the ideal in feminine beauty was looking pregnant. Even a woman who was single was encouraged to look "fertile." One has only to look at the great paintings from the Renaissance through the Victorian era to see that the feminine ideal used to be women who were curvaceous, voluptuous, and generally rounder than today's ideal. This was the original airbrushing, but instead of creating ultrathin and emaciated women, those Renaissance painters portrayed a full-bodied woman as the epitome of sensuality and sexuality. The thin woman ideal emerged in the 1920s, as women's civil rights grew and women began to reject traditional feminine images. Since then, this ideal has taken on a life of its own and is the cause of all sorts of eating disorders in young women. Also, when a society is well fed, thinness denotes self-control or an ethereal abstinence that appears saintly. So thinness became chic in the 1920s, when the industrial revolution was booming and the middle class was well fed and growing.[1]

When John was a young assistant professor at Indiana University, he wanted to take a summer workshop offered by the Kinsey Institute. They agreed to let him in for free if he would run one group session consisting of six men and six women. Most of them were sex therapists. The group discussion was to be stimulated by an initial exercise the Kinsey Institute designed. Each person had to describe how he or she felt about his or her body overall, and then they each had to choose a specific body part and tell the group how they felt about it.

Now John thought this would be a pretty easy group to run, but as he looked at the 12 participants it struck him that this was an unusually attractive group of people. The women were quite beautiful and the men all very handsome. Apparently sex therapists are an attractive bunch. John thought the exercise would end up being a dud, since he imagined each of these attractive people would say, "Look at me, look at how sexy I am, how great I look. I need to pick some part of my body? Well, I love every part of my body. What's not to love?"

It turned out John was wrong—really, really wrong. Every one of these men and women hated their bodies. A woman would say, "I don't like my body. I'm too fat. These are my breasts. I hate them the most. They're too small and they droop too much." The men were just as bad. It seems men are not immune to having painful relationships with their bodies, too.

As a man, you may not be obsessed with the size of your ass, but all men are obsessed with being inadequate (with the size of something else). Sex therapist and lecturer Bernie Zilbergeld, who wrote the bestseller *The New Male Sexuality,* told us that one medical drawing in his book had an enormous impact on most men. It was a drawing of a wide range of erect penises. They were all different and all acceptable, and that fact amazed most men. Most men evaluated their own erections and thought they were inadequate. It is a startling fact that the overwhelming number of customers for drugs like Viagra are young, healthy males, not older men with actual erectile dysfunction. Think about the preoccupation that most men have with the size, shape, and acceptability of their penises and imagine that you felt this insecure about every aspect of your body. Now you have some understanding of how most women feel about their bodies, all the time.

There's so much more, though. Women were chattel for men— the more beautiful and fertile they appeared, the more money was paid for them in the form of a dowry. Women were taught only the domestic arts, and most were not taught to read or write, so how they looked and dressed themselves became their entire identity. That's been going on for 3,000 years—how women look is bred into their bones. They compare themselves to other girls from the minute they are conscious of their gender. And almost always they see themselves as wanting. They feel that how they look is paramount.

The most important part of being a great lover, of being her best ever, is letting her feel your loving appreciation for her body in and out of bed. As we said previously: If she isn't comfortable with her body, she's not going to be comfortable sharing it with you. We'll let you in on a secret: A woman's desire is dependent on her feeling desirable. You can be the greatest sexual Olympian, but if she's not feeling good about her body, she's not going to feel much of anything during your carnal decathlon. Lovemaking starts long before you get into bed—lovemaking begins with your words, your smiles, and your gaze. To put it another way, the greatest sex organ a woman has is her mind. Make her feel your attraction to her, your passion for her, your devotion to her, and you will be a great lover before you raise a finger, flick your tongue, or make your first thrust.

Now that you know the importance of her mind and heart, we can talk about what to do about that wonderland called her body.

★ A woman is exposed to hundreds of ads a day that tell her what her body is supposed to look like. Women rarely measure up to the ideal standard of beauty portrayed by the fashion and entertainment industries. Let her know she is beautiful exactly as she is.

★ A woman's relationship with her body is fragile, and even one "joke" or mean comment about her weight, size, or attractiveness can cut deeply. Heroes never criticize a woman's body.

★ Men can't reverse the constant societal pressures to be thin and beautiful, but men can make any woman feel beautiful.

★ Compliment her. Show her you adore and desire her just as she is.

★ If a woman has a poor body image or believes you don't find her attractive, she will not be comfortable with you sexually.

YOU MIGHT BE A ZERO IF. . .

✖ You criticize a woman's body.

✖ You check out other women when you are with her, or you comment on the body parts of another woman.

✖ You suggest that she go on a diet or start to exercise.

✖ You tell her she does in fact look fat in that outfit. The only correct response is, "You look beautiful in everything you wear."

✖ You fail to make her feel desired, adored, or beautiful.

✖ You compare her looks to other women or past girlfriends.

✖ You treat her like a sexual object rather than a real person.

Chapter 8

HER BODY IS A WONDERLAND

An Anatomy Lesson

i like my body when it is with your body.
it is so quite new a thing.

muscles better and nerves more.

—e. e. cummings

PASSION BEGINS IN the mind. When a woman feels passionate—whether it's about her work, her family, or you—her body comes alive, her emotions are heightened, and she is capable of experiencing an incredible amount of pleasure and having amazing sensual experiences. But this capacity for ecstasy always begins in a woman's mind and heart. They are her most powerful erogenous zones.

To truly know a woman's body you have to first know her mind and heart. That's why we began this book by teaching you how to attune. A woman needs to feel connected to feel desire. She needs to feel emotionally and physically safe with you before she can feel completely safe sexually. She can fake desire. She can even fake an orgasm. But if you're attuned, you will know when she's not really connected—to you or to her body. You can have encyclopedic knowledge of all the specific nerve endings that can pleasure her and drive her into a frenzy, but if you don't first ignite her mind or connect to her heart, those nerve endings are not responsive. They won't ignite. They won't even shoot off a single spark. Nothing. Nada. Zip.

Your job is not only to know her body and what brings her pleasure, but also to know how to help her feel connected and safe enough to be open to pleasure. You want her to be able to tell you what feels good and what doesn't, or what satisfies her and what leaves her wanting. There is a common myth that if a woman doesn't reach orgasm, the man is not a skillful or good lover. That he has failed. This is definitely a myth because ultimately, a woman is responsible for her own sexual pleasure. As Doug's mother once said, "In life, everyone is responsible for their own orgasm." (Wise words from a wise woman.) You, however, are responsible for helping her get there and for understanding how a

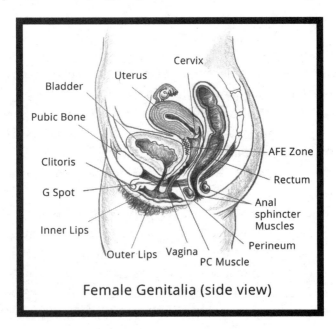

Female Genitalia (side view)

woman's brain and body work when it comes to making love. Because we'll tell you this much—it's not the same as yours. It's also not the same as what you may see in movies, television, or pornography. But we'll get to the "how" in the next chapter. For now, we're going to guide you through the wonders of the female body and explore the basics of female anatomy.

Now most of us took a health class back in the day, but it may be surprising to know that most adult men cannot accurately label a diagram of the female reproductive system. BuzzFeed, a popular online media site, asked its (adult) male readership to label the same female reproductive diagrams given in most junior high health classes. The results were both hilarious and atrocious.[1] It's not surprising that many males are grossly uneducated about the female body; what is surprising is that the BuzzFeed quiz found that so many women also seemed in need of a refresher course. So before we take a trip around the female body and review a few things you may have forgotten that you learned in health class

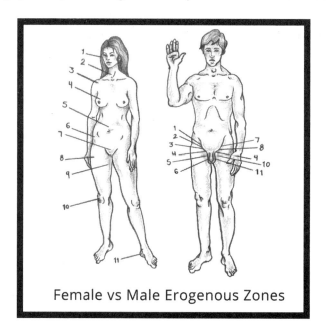

Female vs Male Erogenous Zones

(and a few things that you never learned in health class), we should be perfectly clear on one important point: There is no part of the female reproductive system called the "labia menorah."

If the first diagram is just too clinical for you, the other one gives you the basic differences between the anatomy and erogenous zones of a woman and a man. Consult each diagram as you see fit.

A woman's body and her sexual organs have always been seen as mysterious. A man's sexual organs are out there for the world to see, but a woman's are mostly internal, and most men have spent a lot of time wondering where exactly her parts are located, especially the parts that *are* somewhat mysterious—the G-spot, the clitoris, the A-spot, and now what researchers are calling the U-spot. Imagine researchers coming up with a new "spot" for men. Unfortunately, the spots on a man never change—yet one more reason why the anatomy of a woman can be so confounding. Her body is, without a doubt, a wonderland, so let's take a tour of the hot spots of female sexual anatomy and solve the mystery.

MONS VENERIS. This may sound like the name of a swanky European city, but it is Latin for "Mount of Venus." Still sounds swanky, we know. We call it the "mons" for short, and it's the padded area on top of a woman's pubic bone. In its natural state, it is covered with hair, but with trends in grooming (think Brazilian bikini wax) it may be bare, have a strip of hair, or be groomed into any pattern chosen by a woman. The Brazilians seem to have had a huge cultural impact on both soccer and the mons.

LABIA. This is another Latin word that comes from the word *labium,* meaning lips. As the mons descends below the pubic bone, it separates into two sets of lips—the labia majora (outer lips) and the labia minora (inner lips). The labia majora are longer outer lips that are covered with hair (typically). The labia minora are thin inner lips that are hairless and can vary in color from pink to tan to brown, depending on a woman's skin color. When she is aroused, the labia minora and majora can swell to several times their original size. Think of women who have plastic surgery to plump up the lips on their faces—this is kind of like that, but all natural and without the collagen injections. These swollen lips are a thing of *real* beauty because they mean she is aroused and lubricated, and that is just what you want her to be.

CLITORIS. If you travel up the labia minora back toward where they meet at the mons, you will find the clitoris—or where the clitoris is supposed to be. Finding the clitoris can be somewhat like playing "Where's Waldo?" The clitoris can be small, hidden, and can look like everything else around it. Where the top of the inner lips meet, they form a hood that protects the clitoris. Why does the clitoris need protection? It's not a "hiding out from the mafia in witness protection" kind of thing—it's more of a sensitivity issue that causes the clitoris to need some coverage. The clitoris is full of nerve endings and is extremely sensitive. In fact, the clitoris has as many nerve endings as the head of your penis and is a *lot* smaller. This is why stimulating the clitoris is the surest way to help a woman orgasm. We'll tell you exactly how to approach this bundle of nerves in the next chapter, but for now it's just important that you know it's there and that you know how to find it. When it comes to the clitoris, there is a big difference between Heroes and Zeros. A Hero can find the clitoris, and he's not afraid to ask directions if he gets lost. A Zero wouldn't know a clitoris if it hit him in the face. And that's just sad. Trust us when we say that this is one area where you most definitely do not want to be classified as a Zero. The man every woman wants has a healthy relationship with and respect for the clitoris.

VAGINA. This is where some men get confused. If you think we have been describing the vagina this whole time, you're not alone in your confusion. Technically, to get to the vagina you go south of the clitoris, past the urethra, and make a sharp U-turn at the entrance to the vagina. The vagina is amazing—its walls rest against each other and are made of many folds that allow it to expand and contract to fit around a finger, or a penis, or a baby's head. Did we mention it's amazing? When a vagina is resting (not aroused and just lounging about her day), the front wall is about 2.5 inches long and the back wall is about 3 inches long. When the vagina is not resting (aroused and busily going about her day), the first third of it tightens and gets smaller while the inner two-thirds balloon out. Within the vaginal walls there are many frontiers to explore.

G-SPOT. Apart from the clitoris, this is the other mysterious spot that men wonder about and try their hardest to find. Is there really some magical spot that can drive a woman wild? Do some women have it and others don't? It's been a controversial subject with sex researchers ever since Dr. Ernst Gräfenberg first

COLIN'S GPS WAS TO PROVE LESS THAN USELESS AT FINDING MAUREENS 'G' SPOT

described it in medical literature in 1950. Now you might have thought the *G* stood for gangster or even goddess, but it was named after Dr. Gräfenberg in light of his "discovery." (Although saying Dr. Gräfenberg discovered the G-spot is sort of like saying Columbus discovered America. It's pretty clear that both existed and were familiar to the natives before any man laid claim to their discovery.) Regardless, the G-spot is located about one to two knuckles in from the opening of the vagina, under the pubic bone. It is an area of ridged tissue that swells to about the size of a quarter when a woman is aroused.

A-SPOT AND U-SPOT. If the G-spot is the celebrity guest of the vagina, the A-spot and U-spot are the lesser-known characters who make up the G-spot's entourage. The A-spot is also called the anterior fornix erotic zone (AFE) and was discovered by Chua Chee Ann, MD, of Malaysia. This spot is located 4 to 5 inches into the vagina, between the bladder and the cervix. It's somewhat difficult to reach unless you have fingers like E.T.

The U-spot is a small patch of very sensitive tissue that is found just above the opening to the urethra and along it sides. It

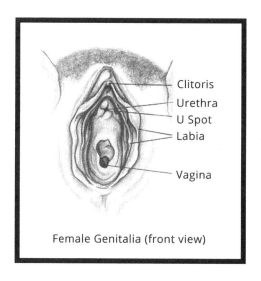

Female Genitalia (front view)

is below the clitoris and is shaped like an upside-down U (thus the name).

Regardless of what letters of the alphabet you give to these various "spots," there is a deeply pleasurable world for you to visit and explore. Not all women are aware of these spots or have felt them during lovemaking. And even if she doesn't know the name of her anterior fornix erotic zone, she is going to know the pleasure she feels when you touch, stroke, and caress these areas the way she likes. We'll get into how to use the various parts of your anatomy to touch her anatomy in the next chapter, but remember that what feels good to one woman may not feel good to another woman.

We can tell you the best attractions to visit when touring a woman's body, but your (and her) experience of these hot spots is going to vary immensely. A woman's body, her arousal, her pleasure, her orgasm, and her experience while making love are subtle and complex. They involve so much more than just her sexual anatomy. That's just a small percentage of what turns her on and gives her pleasure—the wonderland that is the female form.

You can find your partner's own unique spots as you pleasure her and explore her sexual landscape. The key is to tune in to her and let go of any expectations about what she should feel. Just enjoy the sights and sounds of what she does feel.

The 99 Percent

To truly pleasure her, you have to explore the rest of the female anatomy—head to toe. If you think the erogenous zones of a woman are limited to her genitals, think again. She gets turned on when you stroke her hair or kiss her lips, her neck, her breasts, her ears, her shoulders, her thighs, the palm of her hand, or the small of her back. Her skin is sensitive to the slightest touch and the sweetest caress. To truly make love to a woman you have to make love to her whole body with your mind, your eyes, your words, your heart, and your touch. A Hero in the bedroom knows that his pleasure comes from her pleasure. This is the big secret. Take the time to find out what feels good to her and what gives her pleasure, and your pleasure will increase exponentially.

The other big secret to the female anatomy is that there's not a single part of her body that is not an erogenous zone if touched in the right way. In the next chapter we'll tell you how to make passionate love to every inch of her.

★ A woman's mind is her most powerful erogenous zone. She needs to feel physically and emotionally safe and connected with you in order to feel aroused and experience pleasure.

★ The sexual anatomy of a woman is complex. Explore what feels good to her and help her show you what gives her pleasure.

★ Find the clitoris, and if you can't find it, ask for directions.

★ A woman has various spots—G-spot, A-spot, U-spot—that may be highly charged and erotic for her if touched and stroked the right way. Explore the spots that feel good to her, but don't pressure her to feel pleasure in any particular spot. Every woman—and every woman's body—is different.

★ The erogenous zones of a woman are not limited to her genitals. (The same is true for men.) Any part of her body can be a source of extreme pleasure with the right touch. The skin, neck, ears, lips, shoulders, breasts, back, and thighs of a woman can all be erotic.

★ Her pleasure will increase your pleasure.

YOU MIGHT BE A ZERO IF...

✖ You don't make her feel sexually safe by making her feel physically and emotionally safe.

✖ You ignore her mind, lips, neck, shoulders, breasts, thighs, or any other potential pleasure-inducing spot on her body.

✖ You don't touch her slowly and gently.

✖ You ignore the clitoris.

✖ You can't find the clitoris and you don't ask for help.

✖ You think a woman's erogenous zones are all located below the waist.

✖ You think every woman's body is the same and every woman's response to your touch should be the same.

✖ You still ignore the clitoris, even after reading this list.

Chapter 9

BECOMING HER BEST EVER

A Primer on Passionate Sex

*The real lover is the man who can thrill you just
by touching your head or smiling into your eyes—
or just by staring into space.*

—Marilyn Monroe

TO TRULY BE the Hero in a woman's life, you have to be a Hero
both in and out of the bedroom. Here's the catch, though: As we
said earlier, every woman is different. When it comes to making
love, some women like things slow and gentle. Some women like
things fast and hard. And most women want different things at
different times in their day, or cycle, or stage of life. Some women
will be comfortable telling you what turns them on, and others
will leave it up to you to guess what leaves her breathing hard and
quivering in ecstasy. When in doubt, we want you to think of the
porcupine.

When John was an assistant professor at Indiana University,
the famed sex researchers Masters and Johnson had just published their groundbreaking research on human sexual response.
It was 1972, and having grown up in the '50s, John was not used to

direct sex talk. After Masters and Johnson's research was published, many couples came into the clinic asking for help with their sexual problems. John tried hard to be professional, but every time he had to say "penis" or "vagina" he would falter and the words would come out as a barely intelligible stutter: "P-p-p-enis." "V-v-v-v-vagina." Needless to say, these were not words used freely around the dinner table when he was growing up.

Luckily Indiana University was the home of the famous Kinsey Institute for Research in Sex, Gender, and Reproduction. Paul Gebhard, one of the researchers who worked with Kinsey and co-authored the famous *Sexual Behavior of the American Female,* was offering a seminar on sexuality that was made for John and his "stuttering problem."

During the seminar, John had to watch films of just about every animal in the kingdom having sex. He saw elephants doing it. He watched dogs, horses, camels, mice, giraffes, and zebras doing what they did to ensure the survival of their species. He paid close attention to the lions, tigers, and bears—oh my. Most of these sex acts were amazingly fast. None of the animals looked like they were having a whole lot of fun, nor did any of the acts look very romantic.

Until the porcupine.

Now, you can imagine how painful it would be for two porcupines to mate. They are covered in quills, and those quills are razor sharp. The male porcupine has a very interesting dilemma (that perhaps you can relate to). He wants to have sex quickly once he's interested, but if he mounts the female porcupine too soon, and her quills are still up, he is going to get mightily injured. So what he does is he sits down in front of the female porcupine, and he puts his paws on either side of her face. Then he strokes her face very slowly and gently, over and over again. She closes her eyes. Patiently, he continues to stroke her. After a while, he goes behind her and he checks to see if her quills are down. If they aren't, he returns to his former post and keeps stroking her face for as long as it takes. Once her quills are down, it means she is ready for some porcupine loving, and the relationship is consummated, without injury, porcupine style.

The male porcupine is a Hero.

In order for you to be a Hero in the bedroom, you need to emulate the moves of the male porcupine. Stroke her until she's ready, or somebody may end up hurt.

Initiating Sex

According to research, more than 70 percent of both men and women report using indirect strategies to ask for sex. They touch, they snuggle, they kiss. In the Love Lab, we discovered that people make bids for affection and romance in a face-saving way. That is, early in the relationship, partners will test the waters to see whether it's safe to proceed and whether their overture will get rejected. As the relationship matures and people get more comfortable talking about sex, bids for sex become more direct.

So how much sex are people really having? It does seem to be an established fact that men think about sex more often than women. Fifty-four percent of men compared to 19 percent of women think about sex every day or several times a day. In our research of couples' sex lives, we found that, ideally, men want sex four or five times a week, and women one or two times. Men have more explicit sexual fantasies and women have more romantic fantasies. Adolescent males masturbate more than adolescent females, and that trend continues into adulthood. Men in general are more receptive to sex than women are. Generally, we can conclude that the bottom line is that men have fewer prerequisites for sex than women do.

Honestly, how many men have a list of requirements before they are willing to have sex?

Anyone?

The difference between men and women is often expressed this way: Women need to feel emotionally connected to have sex, and men need to have sex to feel emotionally connected. But we think the statement that men have fewer prerequisites than women fits the data better. It partly explains why gay men have the most sex of any type of couple—*two* people with fewer prerequisites. It also partly explains why lesbians have the least sex of any type of couple: Two people with the most prerequisites.

The prerequisites women have aren't always about emotional closeness. Sometimes they are about being exhausted, or distracted, or not feeling well, or a host of other considerations. The evidence is pretty clear that despite all of these confounding factors, men are usually willing to overlook them and have sex anyway. Sexual desire for women is a barometer. If she's not happy, or rested, or healthy, or feeling supported and loved, she's not going to feel a whole lot of sexual desire.

There are also hormonal factors that reduce desire for women while they're breastfeeding (nature's way of spacing children) and during and after menopause. Most women continue to enjoy sex after menopause (as long as they are lubricated enough, either naturally or with the help of topical estrogen). However, even though they enjoy sex, many women don't actively desire it as much as they did before menopause. Though it is difficult, it is important not to take this personally. It's not that she's not attracted to *you* any longer, she's just had a shift in her hormonal mix and may require a little extra persuasion before she says yes. Usually she'll be very glad she did, as the good news is that there is typically no decrease in sexual pleasure with menopause. Chronic illness and many medications (including birth control pills) can also affect a woman's desire. Depression, anxiety, and a past history of sexual abuse can all affect a woman's experience of desire, as well.

TRAUMA AND SEXUAL ABUSE

When a woman has a history of sexual abuse, the most important thing is to let her know you are different than whoever abused her in the past. Survivors of sexual abuse will often pull away at the end of sex, or after you've had an orgasm, and curl up in a ball and express despair. A survivor may also flinch when you touch certain parts of her body, and memories of past trauma can be triggered. Only touch a previously abused woman as long as she is feeling pleasure. As soon as she feels pain or numbness, or is absent, stop whatever touch you are doing. You may be inadvertently touching points on her body that were part of her abuse, and when they are touched again, the memories of the abuse resurface intensely. We call these *enduring vulnerabilities.* It's helpful to speak with your partner about what parts of her body she doesn't want touched and to respect those boundaries to the letter. That way, she'll know you only want to love her and respect her, not use or abuse her. Help her to identify the types of touch she loves. Let her know you are there, and ask her if she'd like to talk about it. Many women who have been abused feel like damaged goods and are worried that you will be repelled. Tell her you are there for her in whatever way she needs, and let her guide you in how she wants to be touched and how to make love to her. Women who have been abused want to heal and reclaim their sexuality. It takes communication and patience on your part.

It is worth mentioning that we are generalizing about women when we say that they have more prerequisites for sex than men do and that many women have reduced desire with menopause. This is certainly not the case for all women, and women at all ages can have strong libidos. We have all worked with couples where the woman had a stronger sex drive than the man. For the guy, this can be wonderful, exhausting, or even threatening.

Interestingly, women agree to sex at the same rate that men do. Psychologists Sandra Byers, PhD, and Larry Heinlein, PhD, conducted a study in which 22 men and 55 women were asked to keep records of their sexual encounters. The research found that males initiated and considered initiating sex more often than women, with cohabiting men initiating more than married. However, there were no differences between men and women in their *responses* to initiations. Both men and women responded positively to initiations or bids for sex about 75 percent of the time. Mostly these initiations were nonverbal. They started with emotional connection, romance, then affection, kissing, caressing, and, if the signals were right, moved on to erotic touch. The bottom line of this research is, *ask her for sex.* You have a 75 percent chance that she'll say yes, assuming all else is going well—she is rested, connected, unstressed, and feeling safe.[1]

Most importantly, don't take it personally if she says no. Zeros get angry or defensive when they are turned down. Heroes say something like, "Baby, you just look so beautiful tonight. Maybe we can find another time when you're feeling more rested." Or, even better, "Thanks for telling me you're not in the mood for sex. What are you in the mood for? Would you like to take a walk, or make popcorn and watch a movie, or just talk, or cuddle?" Think those guys get lucky more often? You bet your boots they do.

Personal Sex

All men want to make love with wild abandon and passion and to be her best lover ever. But the bottom line is, a woman needs to feel close and connected to you in order to have great sex with you. We're talking about great sex, not *okay enough* sex. Any two people can connect body parts, move around, and perform the act of intercourse. The end result will be about as flat and exciting as that last sentence. That kind of sex is impersonal, disconnected, and it leaves you feeling vaguely empty and dissatisfied. Sure, there is the physical satisfaction, but truth be told, this kind of impersonal sex is not that much different from masturbation. In fact, it's worse. After you masturbate, you don't have the awkward task of saying goodbye to yourself. We're going to tell you how to have personal, memorable, and sometimes even ecstatic sex.

Most casual and impersonal sex is some form of mutual masturbation. It's not bad; it's just not great. We're not here to condemn or judge impersonal sex. We realize that some men are just about having as much sex as possible, regardless of the quality. But this is like the difference between pizza that you get because it's cheap and guaranteed to be delivered within 30 minutes and gourmet pizza that takes a little longer but is so tantalizingly delicious it's worth the wait and the effort. Yes, all pizza is pretty good. But you know the real deal when you taste it.

Researcher Meredith Chivers, PhD, discovered what is now known as "the discordant effect." This discordance is the difference between the genitals becoming engorged with blood (a purely physiological measure) and actual desire for sex (a much more psychological/behavioral measure). It might surprise you to know that men, when their genitals become engorged with blood, only experience desire 50 percent of the time. For women, it's only 10 percent. That means that for all men and women, the engorgement rarely means something sexually relevant has just occurred. Interest does not spell desire—especially for women.

The secret to turning physiological interest into actual desire for sex is to connect the mind, the heart, and the genitals. In other words, it's not just about what you do, but also how you do it. This is true whether you are hooking up for the night or spending your wedding night together. You want to be the kind of pizza she wants to have over and over again, not the pizza that was kind of cold and tasted a little like cardboard.

PORN IS NOT SEX

To become a great lover, you have to forget everything you've seen on porn sites. It's not easy to wipe your memory banks. The more you watch porn, the more you want sex that looks like porn. The problem is that porn is all created around a man's fantasy and the frenzy of a man's masturbatory experience. It has nothing to do with what real women want. If you make love like a porn star, you are going to leave your partner pretty unsatisfied.

Are we saying you should never watch pornography? No, we just want to warn you that it can affect your brain and even your erection. Heavy porn use or porn addiction can interfere with a satisfying sex life and satisfying your partner. Here are five signs that you may have a problem and should seek help.

1. You are becoming antisocial.
2. You're keeping your porn watching secret.
3. You lose track of time while watching porn.
4. Porn is interfering with your sex life.
5. You start thinking sex should be like porn.

The main point here is that you need to understand that sex and pornography are about as different as intercourse and masturbation.

So what's the difference between porn and sex?

In porn, women are wet and waiting for sex at all times. This is acting, not reality. **In real sex,** women typically need to be courted, pleased, tantalized, and aroused.

In porn, women worship a man's penis. **In real sex,** most women don't like a penis until they like the man that it is attached to.

In porn, intercourse is about pounding as hard and as fast as possible. **In real sex,** the rhythm of lovemaking varies according to the mood, the moment, and how aroused you become by her arousal.

In porn, women have orgasm after (fake) orgasm and are fully satisfied through intercourse. **In real sex,** only one-third of women orgasm during intercourse alone.

The Art and Science of Lovemaking

Making love to a woman is as much art as science, so like every great artist, you need to have a little inspiration to get started. Keep in mind that the average amount of time that a woman takes to orgasm during masturbation is about 10 minutes, which—big surprise!—is about the same amount of time that it takes a man to orgasm while he's masturbating. In other words, it's not that women need endless foreplay and men don't. Women do not light candles, play romantic music, and take a long time to come when they masturbate. If you have some skills, you can pleasure your partner relatively easily if she's experiencing desire. Every sexual encounter does not need to be a four-course meal. Think of the following sections as a buffet from which you can choose what you want (and what you want to serve her) on any particular night.

The most important thing to remember is that this is supposed to be fun and enjoyable for both of you. There is no need for stress and anxiety—including performance anxiety. You don't need to worry about whether she's aroused enough or your erection is hard enough. There's always something fun to do, whether she's wet or not and whether you're hard or not. The best thing you can do for both of you is enjoy yourself and enjoy your partner. If you're having fun, she will, too. If she's having fun, you will, too. It's one of the best things about sex: What's good for her is good for you, and what's good for you is good for her.

A Pulsating Mind

While a woman is turned on by how a man looks, she is even more turned on by how he speaks, how he acts, how he treats her, how he touches her. If men are porn, women are erotica. Sex for women is a story. Remember that you are writing a story in her mind about her, about you, and about your building passion. The takeaway: Think about sex as something that starts with the way you hold her hand or kiss her lips or even open the door for her. Long before you fall into bed together, you can be creating anticipation. You can text, suggest, flirt, and create a sense of possibility and inevitability. Even long-term couples need to remember to stoke the fires long before they fall into bed at night.

Why does this work? It's the dopamine. Dopamine is the primary neurochemical of the reward system in your brain—it's what causes your partner (or you) to seek rewards. Dopamine gives you the sense that something wonderful is about to happen. The anticipation of reward is the experience, and there is no greater reward, evolutionarily speaking, than expecting great sex. That is the craving. The more aroused she is, the higher her dopamine, and the higher her dopamine, the more she craves something—in this case, you. This is why anticipation is so important. It creates the desire to seek in the brain. Think about how fun it was to play hide-and-seek as a child. We're not suggesting that you play children's games here—just keep your partner anticipating your next text or touch or kiss. Novelty also spikes dopamine, so the more you keep things interesting and avoid pushing the familiar buttons, the better. Dopamine is about wanting and desire, and you want her to want you.

Her Voluptuous Soul

The key to personal, pleasurable, even ecstatic sex is the eyes. When two people look into each other's eyes, they initiate that "social glue" we mentioned earlier. There are few things more intimate than gazing into each other's eyes. We're not talking about a creepy stalker stare. We're talking about gazing passionately and lovingly into a woman's eyes.

One key here is smiling, since the smile is the most important human gesture for demonstrating intention. Remember what we said about making a woman feel safe. Your smile makes her feel safe and lets her know that your intentions are good. You can't fake a smile, though. If you just curl up the corners of your mouth you will look frightening, because your partner can tell a sincere smile from a fake one. A real smile (called a Duchenne smile, after the French anatomist who first noticed the difference) actually comes from the corners of your eyes, not the corners of your mouth. The only way to generate a real smile in these circumstances is to think about the affection and appreciation you feel for your partner. Whether you're loving the one you're with or you've been with the one you're loving for 50 years, you want to look at her with a sense of joy and excitement for what you are about to do together. If you can't sincerely generate those feelings, then maybe you should think again about what you are about to do. Nobody is gazing into each other's eyes in pornography because they're just mutually masturbating each other. It's a fine way to pass the time, but it is not going to be her best ever, or yours. Once trust and connection are established, you are ready for the kiss.

Puckering Up

In Richard Linklater's brilliant movie *Boyhood,* Mason, the main character, is working as a busboy and dishwasher at a restaurant and is flirting with one of his coworkers, who tells him that she won't kiss him. As she leaves the kitchen she tosses over her shoulder, "That doesn't mean I won't blow you." A sign of the times, where blow jobs are even more common than kisses? Possibly, but the truth is that a kiss has always been a sign of real intimacy and in many ways is much more personal than a blow job or many other sexual acts. In the multination study of 70,000 people published in the 2014 book *The Normal Bar,* researchers discovered that people who had great love relationships kissed one another passionately on a regular basis. They also touched one another more often in nonerotic ways, cuddled more often, paid one another more compliments, talked more often, gave one another surprise gifts, and so on, than people who had unhappy love relationships. They stayed good friends. This reinforces our theory that everything positive you do for her is actually foreplay.[2]

On a more scientific note, kissing is also a central part of "mate assessment," according to biological anthropologist Helen Fisher. People can often tell how well they "fit together" when they kiss. Kissing may also play a more physiological role, as saliva seems to contain testosterone, which might increase your partner's sex drive. Men apparently tend to like wetter kisses more than women do, and they may have an ulterior motive. We caution you against being too hot and heavy with your saliva or tongue. The goal is not to drool here, and varying your kisses between passionate open-mouth kisses and featherlight pecks on her lips and at the corners of her mouth will create novelty and avoid her thinking you are trying to drown her.

Your lips and tongue are two of your most powerful sex organs, and you can cover her body with kisses, licks, and love. Just as men want their bodies to be accepted, adored, and even worshipped, so do women, and there is nothing that tells her that you adore her more than kissing her all over and appreciating every inch of her body with your lips.

Kissing her neck (and the nape of her neck) seems to be particularly intimate, as she is vulnerable when she bares her neck for you. As we discussed in the seduction chapter, when a woman bares her neck it's a major sign of interest, and that is the time for you to appreciate the neck that she has entrusted to your lips.

Your Touch Is Electric

Your tongue does not have to do all the work. You have 10 little tongues (or 10 little penises, depending on how you use them)—

your fingers. Sensual touch is often light and suggestive, tantalizing the skin. You can, of course, experiment with different forms of touch, from awakening the skin to massaging the muscles.

When you are approaching a woman's nipples, do so with care and consideration. A woman's nipples are a very powerful erogenous zone and also have lots of emotional associations for her. It is best to approach tenderly, circling around her nipple, both to create anticipation and to make it clear that you don't think a nipple is a switch to be flicked on and off. In fact, do not flick the nipple, or grab her breasts and make honking sounds, or stick your head between her breasts and make motorboat sounds unless you want to find yourself alone on the floor. Breasts are to be cherished. Start with a light and delicate touch, as if there is electricity in your fingers. As anyone who has experienced a static electric shock knows, there is actually a charge in your fingertips. Use your forefinger to gently awaken her breasts. You can also try rolling her nipples between your forefinger and thumb—gently! As she becomes more aroused, she may want you to squeeze her nipples more intensely, but it's always best to approach with gentleness. She'll push your fingers into her breasts if she wants more intense pressure.

Most men have a pretty familiar routine: Step 1, kiss the lips; Step 2, touch the breasts; Step 3, touch the clitoris (maybe) or vagina; and Step 4, insert the penis. A skillful lover doesn't follow any set routine. Think outside the box (pun intended). Remember the children's song, "Head, Shoulders, Knees, and Toes." Be creative and see what areas of her body, apart from her breasts and genitals, can cause her breathing to get heavy, can make her shiver, and cause her to arch her back and press up against you. This is what you're after. Female desire is a beautiful, mysterious thing. Allow yourself to be turned on by her arousal, rather than just your own arousal. Physical communication is as much a two-way street as an intimate conversation. And there is nothing more exciting than a woman arching her pelvis toward yours because her whole body is on fire from your touch.

Look into her eyes. Kiss her deeply. Run your fingers lightly up and down her body. Don't rush. Experience her desire. She will know the difference between you making love to her and you going through a routine with the sole intention of getting her ready to receive your almighty penis.

When you do start thinking within the box, proceed even more gently than with her nipples. The clitoris has the most intense concentration of nerve endings anywhere on her body—or yours. It has as many nerve endings as the entire head of your penis, but compacted into a tiny space smaller than the tip of your pinky finger. In short, it's a Roman candle fireworks display hiding in a tiny fold of skin the size of a pea. You are better off using your softer and more delicate lips than your hard fingers, at least until she is aroused and engorged.

Oral Lovemaking

A man's single greatest tool in his quest to pleasure and satisfy his partner is oral sex. Imagine Gandalf without his staff, Harry Potter without his wand, or James Bond without his tuxedo. Impossible to imagine? Well, that's what you'd be like if you did not avail yourself of your oral abilities. If for any reason you do not like oral sex, we say "Get over it." Man up. If your partner smells strongly, you can bathe together. If you do not like her hair, she may be willing to shave. But keep in mind that you are not burying your nose in her pubic hair, you are using your tongue to lick and flick her clitoris. As you become more of a cunnilingus connoisseur, you can choose to suck and roll her clitoris between your lips. This will drive her crazy. Keep your teeth away from her clitoris, however. This is strictly a job for your tongue and lips. As you did with your hands, see what brings her pleasure. Make love to her with your mouth and tongue and remember that consistent rhythmic pressure is usually what gets all her juices flowing and brings her to peak arousal.

Don't neglect the rest of her while your mouth is busy. Idle hands are not good hands. Caress her, touch her breasts and nipples, see what she likes and what drives her passion to the next level. While you are licking and sucking on her lips and clitoris, you can enter her vagina with your fingers. Try one or two fingers and find where inside her vagina is most pleasurable and sensitive to her. (Study up on the G-spot and A-spot from the anatomy chapter.) Every woman is different and there will be areas that haven't been assigned a letter of the alphabet that will cause her to moan and burn with excitement.

The Rhythm of Life

When it feels like she is at the boiling point and can't stand it any longer, when she seems eager to have you enter her, try rubbing your penis on her clitoris and then slowly, inch by inch, move your penis inside her. Don't rush into full-force thrusting. Tease her a little, pull back, and see how she responds. If she is thrusting against you or her legs are wrapping around your back, she wants you to go deeper. Remember anticipation. Tease her. Tempt her. She will go crazy when you actually do thrust fully inside her.

Keep in mind that the rhythm of intercourse in porn is based on the speed at which a man strokes himself. It's a masturbatory rhythm. In real sex, women may like it hard and fast at times, especially as you both build toward a climax, but your best bet is to work up to the harder and deeper rhythm with softer and slower rhythms until she is well lubricated. Otherwise, she might be rubbed raw.

Find a rhythm that works for her and you. Try varying shallow with deep thrusts, as the variation and novelty of the stimulation will be intense. Try moving from side to side. Experiment with rotating your hips so your penis moves in a circular fashion inside her. Gauge her reactions and see what builds her excitement, what causes it to simmer, and what causes it to boil over. At this point, she might want you to penetrate deeply and to let go with your own pleasure and abandon. Remember that you are not just an objective observer; you should be focusing on your own sensations and pleasure as well. Your pleasure will also stoke hers.

Different positions change the angle and depth of penetration. Depending on your genital size (and hers), you might want to experiment with different positions. With man on top, often called the "missionary position," the higher the woman's legs are, the deeper you will enter her. With the woman on top, she can control the depth and rhythm and leave your hands free to play with her breasts and clitoris. With the man entering from behind, your penis will be angled down against the front wall of her vagina and can stimulate her A-spot.

Lend a Helping Hand

A Hero wants his partner to be satisfied, and we're happy to say that most men want to be Heroes. In one study of 4,000 men, 80 percent judged their sexual satisfaction by whether they had been able to give their partner one or more orgasms. So it is no surprise that in pornography women are moaning and writhing with pleasure during intercourse, having orgasm after (fake) orgasm. In real sex, only 25 percent of women (or less) can orgasm with intercourse alone. Her chances of orgasm during intercourse improve dramatically if her clitoris gets the attention it wants, with fingers (yours or hers) or the help of a sex toy. Certain positions can also help with clitoral stimulation, like having a woman on top and able to rub her clitoris on your pubic bone. Interestingly, her anatomy, and in particular, the distance between her clitoris and vagina, may determine whether or not she can orgasm during intercourse, so please do not take her orgasmic habits personally. Sadly, ten to fifteen percent of women have never had an orgasm. If you can establish trust, connect with her, and give her a hand (or a mouth) with orgasm, you will TRULY be her hero. And it should be noted that women who don't orgasm can still enjoy sex, so don't obsess about "giving" her an orgasm—focus on connecting with her and giving her pleasure. You will still be her hero. This does not mean that they may not enjoy sex, it just means they do not experience orgasm. Since most women who have orgasms during intercourse need to have at least some clitoral stimulation, let's give you some inspiration (and instruction) on the care and feeding of the clitoris.

Imagine trying to have an orgasm without touching the head of your penis. Does that make you cringe? It's the same for a woman and her clitoris. This is why it's so hard for a woman to have an orgasm in the missionary position (man on top)—her clitoris barely receives any action in this position, especially if you are propped upright on your arms. As we mentioned in the anatomy section, a woman's clitoris will swell when she's aroused, so don't just dive into the clitoris and start rubbing away. This will get you—and most importantly, her—nowhere.

When she's aching and arching, it will be easy to find her clitoris. Using your fingers, stroke evenly—not too fast and not too slow. Be subtle. You will be able to tell what she likes, and every woman is different. Experiment with different types of stroking on different areas of the clitoris. You can try different pressures, speeds, and movements. If she pulls back at all, change it up. If she's smiling, moaning, or writhing, chances are good you are doing things right. As a side note, make sure your nails aren't sharp. Trimming your nails or getting a manicure may be the manliest thing you can do for your woman.

Bringing Her to the Boiling Point

How do you know whether she likes what you are doing? Of course, you can always discuss it over a cup of coffee the next morning, but in the heat of passion is not the best time for 20 questions. If her passion is already starting to boil, you will be able to ride the waves of pleasure together.

All arousal begins with the breath, and the first sign that your partner is getting hot and bothered is when her breathing becomes increasingly rapid and shallow. If her nostrils flare or her mouth widens, you are doing something good. If she presses her body toward your hand, tongue, or penis, or if her body quivers, keep doing what you are doing. If she arches her back and is moving her bottom from side to side, she is experiencing great pleasure. If she is well lubricated or if she raises her legs to encircle you, she wants you to enter her. If she presses her thighs together, her pleasure is becoming intense. You may notice some facial expressions that reflect the pleasure down below. If she moves from side to side, she wants you to thrust from side to side. If she arches her body against yours, her pleasure is peaking. If she relaxes, pleasure is filling her body. If her vaginal juices spread down her thighs and buttocks, she is deeply satisfied.

Afterglow

Lovemaking doesn't have to end when she has an orgasm or when you have an orgasm—although it's a natural reflex for men to want to fall asleep after they ejaculate. She may want to keep going or have another orgasm after you've come. You can continue to pleasure her with your fingers (10 little penises), mouth, or, if you are a multiorgasmic man, your still-erect penis. Yes, it is true that men can learn to orgasm before or even without ejaculating—what is often called male multiple orgasms. These multiple orgasms have been studied in the lab by William Hartman, PhD, and his colleague Marilyn Fithian, PhD, of the Center for Marital and Sexual Studies. They tested 33 men who were able to have multiple orgasms—in other words, men who could have two or more orgasms without losing their erections. Doug and Rachel have written several books that discuss how to become a multiorgasmic man, woman, or couple. For the purposes of this discussion, suffice it to say that becoming multiorgasmic can help you become her best ever, especially if she is multiorgasmic, too. If you are not multiorgasmic, after you come you will have a refractory period during which all the pleasure and prayers in the world are not going to get you erect again. The average refractory period for all men is typically a half hour, although for 18-year-old men it can be as short as 15 minutes and for 70-year-old men it can be as long as 20 hours or more.

The period after sex is a source of enormous pleasure for women. They often want to be held, stroked, cuddled, and to continue to feel close. A master lover does not neglect this period of lovemaking, even if it's just for a few minutes of connection and caressing of her skin. Yes, you may want to pass out and go to sleep, and that's fine. Put your arm around her. There's nothing you have to do but make her feel safe and loved.

Hold her. Hold her before sex, during sex, after sex. Hold her when you're dating. Hold her when you're married. Hold her when she's upset. Hold her when she's happy. Hold her when she's scared. Hold her when she feels unworthy of being held, and hold her when she's mad. Hold her every time she needs to be held, and you will always be her best lover ever.

It's as simple as that.

★ Forget everything you ever learned from watching porn.

★ Long before you get into bed together, you can begin to make love to your partner by building anticipation and creating a sense of possibility and inevitability. Text, flirt, suggest, and build passion before you even touch.

★ Every time you are sexual, you tell a story about who you are, who she is, and who you can be together. Make the story amazing.

★ Most men have a pretty familiar routine—kiss the lips, touch the breasts, touch the clitoris (maybe) or vagina, and insert the penis. A skillful lover doesn't follow any set routine. You can make love to every inch of her with your words, lips, tongue, and hands. A Hero doesn't just focus on her breasts and genitals.

★ Oral sex is a must for pleasing and satisfying a woman. If you don't like it—get over it.

★ Most women need clitoral stimulation to have an orgasm. Become best buddies with her clitoris.

★ A Hero also makes love to a woman by holding her after the sex is over. This is a great source of pleasure for women. Making this one last heroic effort (even when you want to go to sleep) will go a long way toward making you her best ever.

YOU MIGHT BE A ZERO IF. . .

✖ You believe sex is all about getting up, getting in, and getting off.

✖ You don't explore a woman's body and read the signs and signals of her arousal.

✖ You think sex should be like porn.

✖ You ignore the clitoris.

✖ You don't take the time to make love to her body and help her get aroused.

✖ You think every woman is the same and follow the same sexual routine with all women.

✖ You don't show affection outside of the bedroom.

✖ You don't believe in oral sex.

✖ You don't hold her after sex.

THE MAN'S GUIDE

PART FIVE

TO WOMEN

Living With a Woman

Chapter 10

LEARN TO FIGHT
LIKE A GIRL

Understanding Women and Conflict

AFTER A FEW weeks of dating, once you've become comfortable with one another, you might start experiencing the roller-coaster ride that commonly accompanies any relationship. Inevitably, there will be twists and turns—otherwise known as conflict. As we mentioned earlier, one of the main things men want in relationships (besides more sex) is less fighting. And believe us when we tell you that the two are intimately related. Despite the myth about make-up sex, fighting puts a definite damper on desire for women. The same is true for men. The good news is that you can learn to fight less and resolve conflict more quickly. And the even better news is that both of these things will generally lead to more sex in your relationship.

Here's the headline: A woman will not have sex with you if she is mad, upset, or feeling like you don't hear, understand, or care about her feelings and whatever it is that is causing her to be upset in the first place (whether it has to do with you or not). You can't bully her out of being sad or mad, and you can't reason her out of being sad or mad. You can't *solve the problem* of her being sad or mad by applying your keen logic, reasoning, or negotiating skills.

This may work at the office. It may work in sports. It may work with the men you play poker with. But it will not work with the woman in your life, and it will save you both a lot of headache and heartache if you accept this inevitable truth right up front.

When conflict happens, a woman wants one thing: a good listener. A woman's goal in conflict is to be better understood by her partner. (This means you.) Problem solving is secondary. Now for men, problem solving is usually primary. They attack a problem with the same shock and awe their ancestors used to attack a wild buffalo, a neighboring tribe, or another hominid who was getting just a little too close to their cave or their woman.

There is no place for shock and awe when you're trying to resolve a conflict with the woman in your life.

Save your shock and awe for the bedroom.

Conflict Happens

Much like a similar sentiment expressed on bumper stickers everywhere, conflict just happens. It doesn't have to have a rhyme or even a reason. Psychologist Paul Ekman, PhD, calls these relationship conflicts "regrettable incidents." Regrettable incidents are inevitable in *all* relationships, even if you have the best, happiest, most joyful relationship in the world. Shit still happens, so conflict still happens.

So what is it that generates regrettable incidents most of the time? Is it conflict about money? Is it conflict about family? Is it conflict about sex? Our research shows that most of the time regrettable incidents arise from absolutely nothing. That's right— there is no particular topic that causes fights most of the time. And despite popular beliefs to the contrary, men and women are not all that different when it comes to feeling anger. Researcher James Averill, PhD, who teaches at the University of Massachusetts, Amherst, had both men and women keep diaries of how

"That's precisely what we are talking about, Bob. You cannot simply play dead anytime Vera raises a difficult issue."

often they got angry. His findings showed that there were no real differences between men and women.[1]

Where the differences lie, according to research, is in how men and women manage their anger. Bottom line, men handle their anger differently. Sandra Thomas from the University of Tennessee led the Women's Anger Study, the first "large-scale, comprehensive, empirical study of the everyday anger of ordinary women." Her research found that the causes of women's anger could be rooted in one or more of three categories: powerlessness, injustice, and the irresponsibility of other people.[2]

So if you are not listening to your woman (or you refuse to relinquish control of the remote), she is going to get angry because she will feel powerless. If you don't treat her as an equal in the decision making process or if you betray her trust, she is going to feel injustice and she is going to get angry. If you don't do your fair share of work around the house or don't show up when you say you are going to (irresponsibility of others), she is going to be angry with you.

Raymond DiGiuseppe, PhD, chair of the psychology department at St. John's University in New York, surveyed 1,300 people and also found that while men and women are not different in how often they get angry, they are different in the ways they experience and express their anger. His research showed that when men are angry they are more likely to use physical aggression, passive aggression, and revenge to handle their anger. He found that women stay angry longer, are less likely to directly express their anger, and become more resentful than men. Women also tended to use indirect aggression rather than direct aggression, meaning that if a woman is angry with you, she is more likely to get silent than to yell at you to your face. (This may or may not be true for the woman in your life.)

So, short of the dawning realization that the woman you are in a relationship with is no longer speaking to you, how do you know when she's angry, and what do Heroes do when a woman is mad at them?

Flood Insurance

We're going to let you in on two secrets we discovered in the Love Lab. First, men get more emotionally flooded and overwhelmed than women do in a conflict situation. And second, once flooded, only men who are able to reduce their heart rates are able to decrease the amount of *criticism, defensiveness, contempt,* and *stonewalling* they contribute to the conflict. These four things are what we call the Four Horsemen of the Apocalypse in a relationship. If you escalate any conflict by responding with criticism, defensiveness, contempt, or stonewalling, there's an 81 percent chance you are ushering in the End of Days for your relationship or marriage.

So what does this look like on any given day? Imagine you and the woman of your dreams are both home after a long day of work. She wants to talk. You want to watch television. You turn on the news or a game, and she wants to tell you about a coworker who unfairly took credit for her big idea on a project. At this point, she's not mad at you, she's mad at this coworker. Perhaps she's feeling powerless to change the situation at work or mad at the injustice of someone else stealing her idea—two of the three areas that research has shown make most women angry.

You aren't listening. You care, but you're tired, thinking of your own day at work, or perhaps you're just hoping for a little rest and relaxation before tomorrow, when you have to slay another dragon. Then you hear the words, "You're not listening to me." Now most men hear this as criticism, rather than what it really is—a need for connection and a *bid for attention* from your woman. After being ignored, this sentence could rapidly turn into, "You *never* listen to me," which is criticism.

If you are unwittingly ushering in the Four Horsemen, your response may be to just ignore this criticism and hope it goes away (another horseman, stonewalling). Or, while never taking your eyes off the television, you could say, "I *am* listening!" (defensiveness). Or your response could be, "I don't listen because every day it's the same thing, blah, blah, blah. Why don't you just quit that job if everyone treats you so horribly?" (contempt). Or, worst of all, "You're always so negative" (criticism), or "I don't listen because you are never logical and always complaining about something" (also contempt).

Does any of this sound familiar? These are all ways of *escalating* conflict. If your goal is to have less conflict with the woman in your life, avoid responding to her with stonewalling, defensiveness, criticism, or contempt. It's self-defeating and a recipe for disaster.

Yet this is what men do naturally when they get emotionally flooded. In this example, the woman wants understanding; she's looking for someone to listen, empathize, and attune. Her discussion of her day didn't start out as a conflict with you. But things can take a rapid turn in this direction when you fail to offer the connection and understanding a woman wants when she is upset about anything.

When you hear anything that sounds like criticism, it can feel like a personal assault, so your primal defense system kicks into gear and you get emotionally flooded. Your heart rate goes up, you are hypervigilant to danger, and you're ready to defend against attack. It's called diffuse physiological arousal (DPA), and in our study of more than 3,000 couples, we found that it is impossible to communicate when in this physiologically aroused state. You know you are flooded if your heart rate is over 100 beats per minute (or 80, if you are in great physical shape). That's the point at which you start secreting adrenaline and launch into DPA. In DPA, you lose access to your sense of humor, cannot listen very well (hearing and peripheral vision are compromised), and tend to repeat yourself (which we call "the summarizing yourself syndrome"). None of these are very good portents for great attunement.

Flooding is the real enemy of constructive dialogue and productive conflict. While flooding has been described before, we now understand it much better because of recent research from the Love Lab. Flooding has three major components: (1) the shock of attack and the need to defend, (2) emotional shutdown, and (3) the inability to self-soothe. We also now know that flooding is the key variable in low-level domestic violence (fights that get out of control and turn into physical aggression).

So there you are, trying to watch the sports channel at the end of the day, and she says, "You never listen to me." If you were a cartoon, your face would get red and steam would start shooting out of your ears. This is what flooding feels like. Adrenaline races through your bloodstream and your instincts tell you to fight or take flight (grab your hat and coat and leave).

Neither strategy works if you're hoping to have a successful relationship with a woman.

So what can you do when you get emotionally flooded? (And even the most enlightened man gets flooded when he feels criticized or attacked.) The Heroes have three simple strategies that have been scientifically proven to reduce their heart rate. The first is to breathe and the second is to count to 10. Breathing and counting to 10 are ways of downregulating or self-soothing. When you take a deep breath you stimulate the vagus nerve, which in turn reduces your heart rate and lowers your blood pressure.

If you still feel no noticeable decrease in your desire to attack your woman verbally (or even physically), then the third strategy is to take a break. There is a difference, however, between taking a break and taking flight. You can't just abandon your woman in the middle of a heated conversation. You have to say something to the effect of, "You know what, I'm having a hard time listening to you right now, and I will come back in 30 minutes so we can continue to talk." If you don't do this, she is going to be hurt by your flight and will worry that you're abandoning her and will never return. Remember, when you are in fight-or-flight mode, when you are physiologically aroused, you are an evolutionarily honed, fine-tuned aggression or flight machine. Anthropologists tell us that men, and even males among our early hominid ancestors, evolved specifically to stay vigilant about danger.

Mostly it was males who protected the clan from predators and enemies. They had to stay vigilant and watchful for signals of danger, and then react quickly. That all required sustained physiological arousal. Staying vigilant means staying on edge and physiologically activated. Today's men are descendants of the males who were good at that stuff. The ones who weren't good at

"It may be evolution to you, but I call it 'avoidance of intimacy issues!'"

this didn't make it. So even though men have evolved, they still maintain vigilance and physiological arousal for long periods once they perceive danger. That is all fine and good when there is real danger. But it isn't too functional when you get your vigilance system aroused by conflict with your partner.

Why isn't it functional? Physiological arousal creates a sort of tunnel vision in which all nonvital bodily functions (like digesting food, supplying blood to your kidneys and genitals, and managing calm and considered thinking) are shut down temporarily so that you can react to the immediate danger. You sacrifice your peripheral vision and hearing. You move carbohydrates stored in your liver as glycogen into your bloodstream as glucose so you can have energy to defend yourself, your family, and your tribe. This adaptive response is great for fighting or fleeing. It's not very good for listening to your partner. It's not very good for maintaining a sense of humor. It's not very good for creative problem solving. It's not very good for practicing empathy. It's not very good for being able to see issues from another perspective. The adaptive response to danger works against you when it is activated during a relationship conflict. So if you didn't feel any empathy for her during a recent argument, you were probably in DPA. You were flooded.

Women, on the other hand, are descendants of females who were able to nurse babies. That required the letdown response, which requires the ability to self-soothe. Your female ancestors did that soothing in part through mutual support and connection with close friends who helped them feel safe. Any woman who has nursed a baby can tell you that tension will disrupt the flow of milk. To facilitate calm and self-soothing, females (even in non-human primate species such as rhesus macaque monkeys) create a social climate that provides the mutual social support necessary for taking care of infants. Rhesus macaques do this by grooming one another, sitting or walking very close to one another, and becoming sensitive to social signals such as facial expressions and even soft vocalizations of distress. This is the opposite of what qualities men were selected for. It's part of the reason that women's social support networks tend to be much better than men's everywhere on the planet.

What are the practical implications of these sex differences? In the heat of a conflict, men are more likely than women to go into the fight-or-flight arousal state, while women are better at self-soothing and wanting to talk things out. That means that women can swim in the same sea of conflict in which most men will drown. What do most men do when they get physiologically aroused? They leave. They stonewall. They are not trying to make matters worse; they are trying to calm down. No matter how advanced men become, they don't make much distinction physiologically between an actual spear being thrown at them and a verbal spear.

Do keep in mind, however, that when women have been

traumatized in the past, either physically, sexually, or emotionally, they too will flood. But their flooding looks different. They may listlessly stare into your eyes, but their eyes are glazed over; they make it look like nobody is home. They are physically present but emotionally absent—this is their way of withdrawing to find safety. This withdrawal may have helped with their trauma when they were younger or more vulnerable, but this emotional "absence" will make moving through conflict nearly impossible in the present. In order to "return" from her own flooding response, she needs to feel safe and to self-soothe, as well. Exhibiting anger toward her in this situation will likely backfire.

The third strategy of taking a break only works if it's a break where you are not thinking about getting even or thinking about being an innocent victim of the alleged spear throwing. If you take a break but spend it thinking about either of these things, you are going to stay physically aroused and emotionally flooded. You need to totally distract yourself.

The break needs to be at least 20 minutes long because it takes that long to diffuse the flooding hormones. If after 20 minutes you are still not calm, then come back to your partner and tell her you need a little more time before responding. In our research, we showed that after conflict a man's heart rate did not lower when he thought about his wife's negative qualities. Surprisingly, it also didn't lower when he spent 20 minutes thinking about his wife's positive qualities. Guess what lowered the heart rate of our participants: reading a magazine. What you need when you're emotionally flooded is a distraction. You need to think about anything but the person you are in conflict with and the conversation that caused the emotional flooding. It's about self-soothing and down-regulating your nervous system. Think about your golf game. Think about baseball. Think about England. Think about anything that has nothing to do with your conflict, and you will soon be able to think clearly. Doing something physical can also help. You can take a walk, read a book, listen to music, go for a run, do some yoga, or meditate.

In our research into domestic violence, we found that couples who experience such violence have no "withdrawal method" or "exit strategy" for conflict. One person blocks the other's exit. Approximately 80 percent of domestic violence stems from the absence of a way to calm down. When the only response in you is a "f**k you," it's in everyone's best interest to take a break. It takes a lot to recover emotionally from harsh words you or your partner say. It's much more efficient to take a break before regrettable (and hard to recover from) words are said. And if you are a man who gets easily physiologically aroused, it's best to talk about it when you are not in the middle of a conflict. Tell your partner, "When I go into fight-or-flight, I say horrible things. I want to stop doing that, and here's my plan to not do that." Create a break ritual so your partner knows what's up and has some idea about what you are going through when you are in the middle of a conflict.

This is what the Heroes do. The Zeros revert to their less-evolved selves and stay in the middle of things, adding fuel to the fire and watching while the relationship burns down around them.

There Will Be Issues

Living with a woman and being in a relationship with a woman will not always be about love, passion, and harmony. There will be issues. Approximately 40 percent of the time, when a woman brings up an issue, men have no clue what she is talking about. We discovered this in the Love Lab, but we also discovered what Heroes do. Heroes do not get defensive. They realize that when a woman is in pain over something, she will not always say so, and that pain may sometimes come out as a criticism. It may feel like a personal attack, but the men who are great at being in relationships will try and find out what is going on underneath the complaint, or the issue, or the criticism. A Hero tries to find out where it hurts, and he does so by asking one or more of the following three important questions:

1. What do you need?
2. What are you concerned about?
3. What are you feeling?

So many of the clients that we have seen have turned away from conflict and in doing so have turned away from their partners. You do not want to leave your partner in a state of pain, and if you avoid or escalate the conflict, each one of these instances becomes a stone in your shoe. Eventually you cannot walk together anymore. Eventually your relationship will end. In short, you can't ignore your partner's pain.

If the woman in your life is criticizing you, or complaining, or bringing up yet another issue she has with you, at the heart of it she wants to be closer, or feel safer, or trust you more. Remember the number one trait she is looking for is trustworthiness. She needs to know that you are on the same team—it's not you versus her. It's not your time versus time spent with her. If she's angry, it means there is something that's making her feel powerless, or some situation that feels unfair, or something that is making her feel like you are not taking responsibility for your part of the relationship. Sometimes it can be an emotional issue and other times a practical issue. At the core of it, you need to keep the agreements you make. Whether that agreement is to be faithful or to pick up your dirty socks—it all matters.

A true Hero in a relationship knows that he needs to listen to his partner. Listen to her needs. Listen to her fears. Listen to her pain. And he needs to learn how to listen just as hard to what she's not saying. Yes, all men want approval from the women in their lives, and it can hurt when you feel criticized or attacked. Everyone makes mistakes, and the women in your life will have feelings about the mistakes you make.

But here's a little secret learned in the Love Lab: The way you respond to your partner in times when there's no conflict and the quality of the friendship between you are what will make a woman less critical and more likely to give you the benefit of the doubt when issues do arise. Investing in the nonconflict time is like money in the bank. It will make times of conflict go a lot smoother and happen less frequently.

Your job as a man is to learn to downregulate your reactivity when she has strong feelings or criticisms. This means you don't get aggressive, try to intimidate, or tell her where she can shove her criticism. And it also doesn't mean you say, "Yes, dear . . ." and bend over and take it. It means you need to be strong enough to listen—really listen—and when necessary take a break in order to calmly respond. Then you man up to the job of finding out why your girlfriend or wife is in pain and what you can do about it. You don't lose your power when you do this—you demonstrate your true power. You also get to have an amazing woman who feels safe with you, who loves you, and who will stay by your side and help fight against whatever life throws at you.

★ Conflict happens—even in the best of relationships.

★ Men and women both get angry with the same frequency, but differ in how they manage their anger.

★ Women get angry because of powerlessness, injustice, or the irresponsibility of others.

★ Men get more physiologically aroused during conflict than women do. This makes men less able to handle conflict with humor, empathy, and understanding.

★ Men are evolutionarily wired to be hypervigilant, aggressive, and to go on the attack if they are being threatened.

★ You can learn to downregulate your anger by remembering to breathe, counting to 10, and taking a break.

★ If your partner is criticizing you, she is in pain. Your job is to find out the source of her pain by asking three questions: 1. What do you need?
                       2. What are you concerned about?
                       3. What are you feeling?

YOU MIGHT BE A ZERO IF. . .

✘ You don't recognize the signs of diffuse physiological arousal (DPA) and don't take action to downregulate before entering into conflict.

✘ You believe that you should always attack when you feel you are threatened.

✘ You resort to verbal or physical abuse when faced with relationship conflict.

✘ You ignore the pain that underlies a woman's criticism or issue with you.

✘ You respond to your partner's complaints or issues by ignoring her, criticizing her, showing contempt for her feelings, or being defensive of your own actions.

✘ You blame others for your anger and heated responses.

✘ You don't keep the agreements you have made in your relationship.

Chapter 11

WHY DOES IT TAKE SO LONG TO BUY A PAIR OF SHOES?

(Understanding the Evolutionary Importance of Shopping)

WHILE THERE ARE some women who don't enjoy shopping, the vast majority of women do. Many men find the way women shop frustrating, and while it may seem cliché, shopping really is a common source of conflict between men and women. You cannot change this evolutionary trait in women, so there's no use getting frustrated about it. By understanding it better, you can learn to avoid the headache of conflict. Remember your goal: harmony, and that comes from being attuned (there's that word again) to how she's different from you.

Since humans first lived in caves and in tribes, women have foraged for food, and they have never known what they might find. In many ancient tribes, the members relied on the women to take their baskets, strap on their babies, and go out and forage. For firewood. For berries and nuts. For roots. For leaves to make tea. For medicinal plants.

All day long—foraging, foraging, and more foraging.

There was a lot of pressure on women back in 8000 BC. Foraging required a great deal of knowledge. Women had to uphold the "gather" end of the hunter-gatherer relationship. Even back then, women had to rely on other women to help; no one liked to gather alone. The women set out each day, never knowing what they might return with, but they knew there had to be a lot of it, it had to be edible, and most importantly, it could not be poisonous. The tribe relied on them to accomplish these Herculean missions every day. That requires a great memory and attention to detail. It is still true that women have better memories than men do.

So what does all of this have to do with women and shopping? From an evolutionary standpoint, we were selected from women who had to develop a keen memory for detail and be good foragers. The first women had to brave the wild and look for firewood, food, drink, and medicine. They looked for things they could use to adorn themselves to look attractive, things they could use to adorn their dwellings to make them more comfortable, and materials that could be used for clothing to keep the family warm. The well-being of the tribe depended on the women and their foraging skills, their memories, and their creativity, all of which evolved so they could bring back the gifts of their foraging and make life better in the tribe. The men hunted, the women gathered, and each had to be really good at what they did in order for the other to survive.

Humans no longer live in caves, but when a woman goes shopping she still takes her basket and sets out to use her creativity and her keen memory to bring back presents for the tribe—food, drink, clothing, medicine, and things to adorn herself, her family, and the "cave."

In the play *Defending the Caveman,* comedian Rob Becker writes that when a man goes shopping he hunts for a particular thing he needs, such as a pair of underwear. He shops like he is hunting for game. He sets out to hunt that one pair of underwear with efficiency and determination. He has a plan of attack. He kills the one pair of underwear, and then he's done and back home quickly with his "kill."

On the other hand, a woman goes forth with her basket to see what there is. She is bringing back things for her family, for her home. She doesn't know what she's going to find, but there is a method and an art to her gathering. Unlike the hunting process, the gathering process is a social endeavor. It's entirely different, and it requires different skills.

The most important skill for the ancient forager was a keen memory, as survival depended on being able to remember which were the poison berries and which were the edible berries. A recent study found that women are better than men at remembering objects. Researchers created a room that could be featured on a television show about hoarding. It had about 100 different everyday objects on shelves, on the floor, on tables, and piled in the corners. They then put different men in the room with the only instruction being, "Wait here." After 20 minutes, they brought each subject into another room and had him write down everything he remembered seeing in the room he had just spent 20 minutes waiting in. The number of objects the men remembered correctly: about 7 items, on average. The researchers then performed the same experiment with female subjects. The women were able to remember about 20 items, on average—a huge difference, almost three times as many.

Back when the feminist movement was first taking off, Eleanor Maccoby and Carol Jacklin coauthored *The Psychology of Sex Differences*. This book strived to make the important point that, by and large, men and women were the same, and it sought to debunk stereotypes about any differences in cognition, socialization, and other aspects of the psychology of men and women. Maccoby and Jacklin reviewed a lot of studies on memory and concluded there were no real differences. But some 30-odd years later, one of the most famous female psychologists, Elizabeth Loftus, PhD, whose area of specialty is memory, reviewed the same studies as Maccoby and Jacklin, along with approximately 20 more studies that had been done since *The Psychology of Sex Differences* was written. Her findings? Women's memories are superior to men's memories, and this is especially true when what's being remembered has any kind of social context.

From an evolutionary standpoint, this holds true. Remember when we told you about the female brain's amazing ability to recall a first kiss? Modern women, who make 85 percent of the buying decisions for a household,[1] need to have prodigious memories to know what to shop for, what prices are best, where to find exactly what they're looking for, and myriad other factors that contribute to shopping-foraging. Oh, that color will go with something else in my closet. Oh, my son could really use this pair of sweatpants. Oh, my husband would love this book. Women have the ability to keep track of all these details.

Shopping is a social activity, and one quite dependent on relationships. Savvy brand managers know that women are more likely to spend their money with people and brands that they have a relationship with.[2] When a woman goes shopping, she may bring her friends with her, or she may have relationships with the people who own or work in the stores she frequents. Women have a "tend and befriend" way about them, and where most men wouldn't think of discussing personal issues with the guy they buy their underwear from, women are likely to know about the sales clerk's relationship status, her family struggles, and her work dreams.

Yes, it can make for some long shopping trips, but this is one of the things men love about women: They have the unique ability to form relationships, even while shopping. Because of these differences between men and women, men typically take far less

Hell was exactly as he had imagined it.

time when they shop. This time difference frustrates many men.

British researchers conducted a shopping study of 2,000 men and women and found that men last for approximately 26 minutes[3] of shopping with their partners before they want to stick a coat hanger in their right eyeball rather than spend another second outside a dressing room. (The coat hanger in the eyeball wasn't part of the study, but we added that to describe our male friends' own feelings while shopping with women.)

Germany seems to have things figured out with the creation of *Mannergartens* in their malls. These spaces are designed exclusively as places where men can wait while women shop. For a few euros, a man gets two beers, men's magazines, a television tuned to the sports channel, and even a model railway car. Apparently the French have followed suit, although they call their men zones *garderies,* which in English means nursery school. You might be offended, but keep in mind that they also serve beer.

Shopping and Identity

A woman's identity has for eons been defined by what she wears and how she looks. This identity, this preoccupation with appearance by women, is not a fantasy in her head or something completely invented by Madison Avenue. In a long-term study of marital success, psychologists Peter Bentler, PhD, and Michael Newcomb, PhD, found that what best predicted whether marriages would last was, believe it or not, a woman's clothes-consciousness.[4] The grim reality is that if she looks good, she will not only attract a partner, but also keep him.

For millennia, the evaluation of women has been based on their attractiveness to men, mostly on how sexy they look. When women shop, it's typically for clothes, cosmetics, and jewelry, and inevitably this is about appearance. Women compete to look great the same way men compete in their jobs or in sports. Women feel they must prove themselves because they subconsciously believe they won't earn a man's love and commitment if they are not deemed attractive. Then, without consciously realizing it, they worry that they won't have a chance to procreate and continue their genetic line. So for women, shopping is a matter of personal and genetic survival. If she takes longer to select her clothes, that's because for her it really is a matter of life and death.

WHY YOU LOVE WOMEN IN HIGH HEELS

Anthropologist Helen Fisher says that when women wear high heels it simulates the courting posture, called *lordosis*, of most mammals. High heels arch the back and thrust out the buttocks, which in the animal kingdom is the universal symbol of sexual readiness.

Why does all this matter? It matters because when you understand the evolutionary drive connected to shopping, you can save yourself a lot of headache and avoid some of that conflict we mentioned in the last chapter. Don't criticize her for shopping. Don't judge her. And most importantly, if you hate to shop, don't go with her.

Most (but not all) women love to shop.

Most (but not all) men do not love to shop.

Embrace the difference. If you can understand that for women shopping is a positive, artistic, and creative experience that is evolutionarily hardwired into their DNA, you can stop fighting this battle with the women in your life. Living with a woman is sometimes about picking your battles, and this battle is one you will not win.

Man up. Bring a book or your iPod. Catch up on e-mail. Find an arcade. And hope she buys you something great. Nobody wants to end up poisoned, so let her practice her foraging skills.

CHEAT SHEET for HEROES

★ Shopping is in a woman's DNA. Women have had to be good foragers since the dawn of time. Lives depended on it.

★ Most, but not all, women love to shop. It is an expression of their creativity and a positive and social experience for them.

★ Women make about 85 percent of the buying decisions for the household.

★ Shopping requires a keen memory, and women have better memories than men.

★ Men shop the way their ancestors hunted—get in, make the kill, get out. Women connect and create relationships around their shopping.

★ If you hate to shop, don't go.

★ Research shows that the degree to which a woman is clothes-conscious is a long-term predictor of marital success.

★ Don't complain if she spends a lot of time shopping for shoes—specifically high heels. Trust us on this one, and read "Why You Love Women in High Heels" in this chapter.

YOU MIGHT BE A ZERO IF. . .

✘ You don't understand a woman's relationship to shopping.

✘ You judge or criticize her for shopping.

✘ You think she should shop the way you shop—get in and get out.

✘ You criticize her purchases or appearance.

✘ You hate shopping but you go along anyway and make her miserable.

✘ You assume all women love to shop. Every woman is different, even when it comes to shopping.

Chapter 12

BEST FRIENDS FOREVER

Understanding Women and Friendship

IF YOU'VE ENTERED into a serious relationship with a woman, the truth is, you've also entered into a relationship with her friends. Let's hope they like you, because if they don't, your life is not going to be pleasant. There's no doubt that women seem to have this friendship thing down to a science, and it's an area where most men are found lacking. Sure men have friends, even some good friends, but it is rare that a man's experience with friendship is anything close to women's. Men don't often have slumber parties with other male friends. They don't whisper and cuddle with each other. Men wouldn't think of walking down the street holding hands with each other (although in many parts of the world, they do). Men don't call their guy friends baby, or sweetie, or honey. They're not affectionate with other male friends the way women are with their friends, although the bro hug is starting to change that a little bit. While not all women relate to their friends this way, it is much more common in female friendships than male friendships. And let's face it, sometimes even the most enlightened male gets either a little jealous of the female friends his partner has, or—if he's being really *honest*— even a little threatened.

Humorist Dave Barry joked about getting together once a year with a couple both he and his wife were friends with. The two women would go off together, and the two men would watch the playoffs on TV and chat every now and then, getting emotional only when they ordered and ate the pizza. On the car ride back home after one particular visit his wife said, "Isn't it amazing how well Harry has adjusted to having his leg amputated last year?" Harry hadn't even mentioned it, so Barry had no idea what his wife was talking about, but he pretended that he and Harry had had a long talk about that.

What exactly are they talking about?

Why do they travel in packs?

Why do they need to be with each other so much?

Why do they go to the ladies' room together even if one of them doesn't have to go?

As it turns out, there is something that women get from their female friends that they can't get from you. You can attune with your partner night and day, and this is great for your relationship, but women still need the company of other women and the support that goes along with it. This is what she gets from her female friends that she can't get from you, and it's crucial. You want the woman you're with to be the most she can be—happy, fulfilled, and satisfied. For this, she needs social support from other women. Period.

It's also important for her health.

In 2006, the *Journal of Clinical Oncology* published the results of a study that investigated the social networks of approximately 3,000 nurses with breast cancer.[1] Women who did not have a lot of friends or who were socially isolated were two times more likely to die from their breast cancer than those who had close friendships. These women also had a 66 percent increased risk of dying prematurely from any cause. The nurses with breast cancer who had 10 or more friends were four times more likely to survive having cancer. Friendships were the single most important factor for these women—even more important than having a spouse, which showed no benefit or effect on cancer survival rates.

Amazingly, it's the opposite for men. Men *need* a woman to stay alive.

University of California, Berkeley psychologist Len Syme, PhD, and his student Lisa Berkman wanted to know what factors predict longevity, all things considered. Syme and Berkman conducted the famous Alameda County Study of about 9,000 people.[2] They measured a huge number of factors in people's lives and then returned 9 years later and examined who was still alive and who had died. This is a very reliable factor to measure, since social scientists can usually acquire accurate death information.

What amazed the world about Berkman and Syme's results was that what determined whether people would eventually wind up alive or dead at an early age was not cholesterol, or exercise, or diet, but the quality of their most personal relationships in life. Interestingly, what determined whether men would die younger was whether or not they were married, whereas for women it was their friendships with other women that determined their longevity. Subsequent research by Lois Verbrugge, PhD, a researcher from the University of Michigan, has shown that the quality of a marriage also helped determine both women's and men's longevity.

So if you want to live a long time, stay with your partner and maintain happiness in your relationship. If you want your partner to live a long time, encourage her to nurture her female friendships.

The life you save may be your own.

Tending and Befriending

There is an evolutionary basis for why women form such close friendships. Much of their survival in the hunter-gatherer era was based on the ability to "affiliate" within the tribe. A woman's relationship with other females determined her safety and well-being and also her children's social status. The more female relationships she had and maintained, the higher the status of her children.

Affiliation with others in the tribe reduced a woman's vulnerability and that of her offspring. It was the woman's responsibility to build a large social network—it meant more resources were shared. If you were the hunter and you came home without any meat, the larger the social network built by your mate, the more likely it was that your family would eat.

The affiliations of females are important in organizing many societies. In fact, among rhesus macaque monkeys, a male's social status and power are determined by who his mother is. Females, not males, determine the social hierarchy of the group. Evolutionary biology tells us that females should have more developed attachment and affiliation systems than males.

You see this today when women organize meals to bring to a new mother or to someone in mourning. Women had the ability to mobilize social support in prehistoric times, and they have that ability (far more so than men do) today.

Female primates also form groups that they depend on to help them survive when they're threatened by larger predators or other male primates. These female primates solidify their social network, and therefore their safety, by spending a lot of time grooming each other.[3] With primates, how often a female is groomed by other females is an indicator of her status and a predictor of how likely she is to be attacked by a predator.[4] The more females she is bonded with, the more likely these females will come to her aid. Now we're not going to make the direct association with modern day females getting their nails or hair done together (since there is not likely to be a predator at the beauty salon), but the idea is similar. Women support each other, and women bond with each other, and while it may no longer be necessary for their physical survival, it is still necessary for their emotional survival.

As pointed out by UCLA researcher Shelly Taylor, PhD, in times of stress, rather than the male fight-or-flight response we discussed in the chapter on conflict, women are more likely to "tend and befriend." This tending and befriending releases oxytocin, which lowers the stress response in women.[5] So if she's upset and turns to caretaking or to her female friends, there is a biochemical reason for this. In other words, don't fight it, don't question it, and try to support it. "Sure, honey, I'll take the kids so you can have time with your friends." Everyone needs time with friends, but for women it's an evolutionary and biological *necessity*.

What Are They Talking About?

You see her with her girlfriends, and they are all huddled up in a group talking. You hear them on the phone—talking. You see them going to the bathroom together—presumably to talk. Just what is it they have to talk about?

The answer? Everything. Women rely on social support from each other in a way that men don't.

Sociologist and professor at Barnard College Mirra Komarovsky, PhD, in her classic study of blue-collar marriages, reported that for most men, their wives were their only confidantes.[6] The only area they didn't talk about with their wives was their job stress. Women, on the other hand, had many areas they didn't talk about with their husbands. Women said that they discussed most personal matters with their girlfriends or female relatives, not with their husbands. You may rely on her as your primary support system, while she very likely has a vast and intricate social network (hopefully) that is ready to stand by her side in case of a predator, share responsibilities and resources, and even groom her, if needed.

Women and their friends are amazing.

Now you may be feeling a little bit left out. Here you are, working hard to attune, learning to turn toward her, empathize, understand, give her your attention, listen when she's in pain, downregulate when there's conflict—so why does she still need all this time and attention from her female friends?

The answer is that even the best of relationships can't give a woman *everything* she needs. The quality of your friendship is important to your relationship, but the quality of her friendships with other women is also important to your relationship.

Dr. Lois Verbugge, a researcher from the University of Michigan, has found that both men and women get health benefits from a marriage, but women only get the health benefits if they are happily married. Men get benefits even if they are unhappy in a relationship (though they get even more if they are happily married). So there is much you can do to ensure that your woman is happy in your relationship.[7] That's what this entire book is about—understanding what women want and need. And here's the good news: You don't have to do it alone.

Female friends are just as much a support for *you* as they are for her because they are also there to listen to her when she needs someone to listen. They are also there to help her handle the big emotions she is going to have at times. They are another voice helping her make decisions and another resource to help her figure out just how she feels, what she wants, and what she needs in life.

A Hero isn't threatened by this. He doesn't resent her friends, and he doesn't try to control who she sees or spends time with. In

MALE FRIENDS

If the woman in your life has a lot of guy friends—or even worse, one close guy friend—it can be challenging. You know how often you think of sex, so you imagine he is thinking of sex. With her. Let's face it, you're suspicious of your partner's male friends. Do they have a hidden agenda, and does that agenda include getting her into bed? Maybe. Maybe not. Men and women can be friends, and they can even be close friends and a source of support for one another. One of the ways that friendships slip into affairs is when a woman starts complaining to her male friends about her relationship. Ask her for reassurance when you need it, and ask her to please not discuss with her male friend any problems that may come up in your relationship, and instead to come to you directly. We'll discuss this further in the chapter on affair-proofing your relationship.

our research into domestic violence, one common denominator among some violent men was that the man felt jealous of the woman's female friends. When these men felt threatened, they attempted to limit and control their partners' social contacts and to isolate them from their friends.

If you find yourself feeling jealous of the time your partner spends with her friends, share your feelings with her. Tell her that you miss her and want to spend more time with her. Don't get angry about it. Most women understand connecting, and if you let her know you need to connect more, she will understand. People have an unlimited capacity to love. She can love you and love her friends.

If you are in a relationship with a woman who doesn't have a whole lot of female friends—perhaps she has been hurt by female friends in the past, or she doesn't trust women, or she just doesn't meet a lot of women—encourage her to reach out and find a women's group. Her happiness depends on it. Her health depends on it. And the long-term success of your relationship depends on it. Female friendship is powerful.

Don't fear it. Don't dismiss it. Don't interfere with it. (Trust us on this one.) And if you still don't understand it, call one of your male friends, invite him to lunch, and talk about it.

You also might want to consider a men's group.

Best friends aren't just for girls.

- ★ Women are more socially connected than men.

- ★ Female humans and primates form social groups to ensure their survival and the survival of their offspring.

- ★ Women tend and befriend when experiencing stress, and this releases oxytocin and reduces their stress response.

- ★ The more friends a woman has, the more health benefits she experiences.

- ★ Women who are socially isolated have a 66 percent increased risk of dying prematurely from any cause.

- ★ Men typically turn to their wives or partners for their social support, but women typically turn to their female friends.

- ★ A hallmark of domestic violence is a man feeling threatened by a woman's friends and attempting to control or limit a woman's social contacts, or to isolate her socially.

- ★ Think of your partner's female friends as supporting you in supporting your partner.

- ★ Encourage your partner to join a women's group or seek out friends if she feels she is lacking in female friendships.

- ★ You live longer if you are married or have a long-term partner. She lives longer if she has female friends. You live longer if she lives longer. Encourage her female friendships.

- ★ Women have a huge capacity for friendship and a need to connect with others, as well as an unlimited capacity for love.

YOU MIGHT BE A ZERO IF...

- ✖ You resent your partner's female friendships.

- ✖ You are jealous of her friends.

- ✖ You try to limit or control her contact with her friends.

- ✖ You judge or criticize her friends.

- ✖ You ignore the need she has for female relationships.

- ✖ You immediately assume the worst of any of her male friends.

- ✖ You have no friends.

THE MAN'S GUIDE

PART SIX

TO WOMEN

Loving a
Woman for
a Lifetime

Chapter 13

IS SHE THE ONE?

Understanding Women and Commitment

It takes more than just a good-looking body.
You've got to have the heart and soul to go with it.

—Epictetus

OFTEN YOU WILL hear men who have been happily married for years say that when they met their spouse they just *knew* she was the one. For some it was her smile, for others her smell, and for others an intangible feeling of rightness, of being "home." For John, "It wasn't that Julie was the most beautiful woman I had ever known, or the richest, or that she was free of conflict and agreeable all the time. It was a certain indescribable quality; she was an outlier among all the women I had dated. She was just different, and it was that difference that made me know for sure that she was the one for me." Doug says, "With Rachel, it was her laugh. I heard her laugh before I ever saw her face, and this will sound odd but that laugh spoke to me. She laughed and I felt it in my body. There was such joy and freedom in her laughter. After 30 years, I am very proud of the laugh lines on her face that I'm responsible for."

"I hope you don't mind, but our first date is going so well, I'm changing my status to, 'In a deep and meaningful relationship.'"

www.cartoonstock.com

Now this doesn't mean that the minute you meet someone who you know is the one you just sail off into the sunset or ride away on your white horse and live happily ever after. You still have to get to know each other. You still go through the stages of love. You still have to make a choice to be in a relationship. You still have ups and downs and days when the other person bugs you. This is called being in a relationship—and whether you know she's the one after you hear her laugh or after 3 or 4 years of dating, eventually you either know that this is the woman you want to commit to or you know that she isn't the one. You can't force commitment. We know from the Love Lab that while we can teach couples all the skills necessary to communicate, deal with conflict, show love and affection, express emotion, and navigate power struggles, if there isn't an inherent "rightness" to the person, no skill set will make up for that. In over 40 years of research and work with couples, we have come to believe that you can't make it work with just anybody.

Contrary to popular perception and gender stereotypes, men want commitment just as much as women do. Sometimes it takes them longer to get there, and sometimes they have more ambivalence about it—two different evolutionary strategies at play—but research suggests that most men are (eventually) as interested in finding "the one" as women are.

Some women.

Not all women want the white picket fence, 2.2 children, and to usher (read trap) you into marriage and commitment as soon after the first date as possible. This is an old and tired stereotype. Today, women have options. Lots and lots of options. And the roles of men and women have changed dramatically during the last 100 years. Similarly, not all men just want to sleep with as many women as possible, never get married, and die in their Hugh Hefner silk robe after a long night of debauchery with 12 blonde nymphomaniacs. (Okay, maybe they want this just a little.) But in reality, not in fantasy, the research suggests that men eventually want meaningful and committed relationships just as much as women do. But if you happen to want to be buried in your best silk robe while 12 blonde nymphomaniacs weep at your graveside, more power to you. This chapter on commitment is probably not for you—yet.

Three Stages of Love

As we discussed in the chapter on reading a woman's true profile, at the beginning of relationships you are in the first stage of love (or lust), called limerence. During this stage you are in a state of chemical confusion and constant oxytocin overdose. This heady cocktail of infatuation is made up of oxytocin, dopamine, phenylethylamine (PEA), testosterone, estrogen, serotonin, and dehydroepiandrosterone (DHEA). You can't eat, you can't sleep, you can't stop obsessively thinking about your partner, you are crazy excited, head over heels in love, and you may find yourself doing some wild things—and the same may be true for whoever the lucky girl is who sets off this cascade of hormones and other chemicals in your body. You can date 100 girls and not have your highly selective limerence switch flipped, but the 101st girl who shows up may just be the one who smells right, feels right, looks right, tastes right, and moves right, and suddenly you are drowning in limerence. It's what drives us to bond, to attach, and to mate. Evolution doesn't care about whether a person is kind or not, it just drives us to reproduce for the best genetic outcome. Being in limerence feels amazing—but only if you have also set off this hormonal cascade in the woman who has set it off in you. If you're in limerence and she has you in the friend zone, this may drive you crazy, but you can't really do anything about it (although you will try and probably cause yourself a lot of misery). And if she is in limerence and you are not, this can make her crazy and miserable as well. One-sided limerence has caused both men and women to be obsessive, manipulative, and crazy enough to hide in the bushes outside their beloved's house. This biochemistry is very selective. When both of you are in limerence, it feels remarkable, wonderful—like the best drug in the world that can't be prescribed, grown, or sold on a street corner. But while you are both under the influence is not the time to make a long-term commitment. This is not the time to rush off to a wedding chapel in Vegas and get married because you think she's the one. It's great to be in love, but remember that oxytocin lowers your fear response and can also make you trust someone even when there are red flags popping up and neon signs that are flashing "dangerous curves ahead." Oxytocin can make you blind to these obvious signals.

This first limerence stage of love doesn't happen everywhere on the planet, especially where marriages are arranged. However, even in these cultures anthropologists have found that quite a lot of selection may actually be going on. Two families in India, for example, may arrange for their son and daughter to meet alone (while the families are in the other room), but if the woman doesn't like the man, she may change to the yellow sari instead of the blue one. A similar signal may have been arranged for him. If either party opts out, the families call it quits, attributing the mismatch to ill-fated horoscopes. Then another potential match is set up. Limerence is neither necessary nor sufficient for a lifetime of love.

During the second stage of love, you start to come down from this hormonal love drug and the haze begins to clear. You start to see the red flags that you ignored before. Stage two is all about building trust. This stage usually takes place during the first couple years of a relationship and as you progress toward living together. The evolutionary drive in this stage is about reproductive care. If evolutionary biology tells us that stage one is about finding the best genetic fit for mating, stage two is about finding out who will help you care for your offspring—whether you are consciously planning to have children or not. (Biology doesn't care about what you *think*.)

What this looks like is trust. Will she be there for me? Will he be there for me? In stage two, many of the qualities that first attracted you to someone may become a source of annoyance or concern. You loved that she was so shy, but now you wish she were more outgoing and wanted to do more things. She loved that you were committed to playing football every Sunday with your buddies, but now she wonders about what happens when she really needs you on a particular Sunday. All of the arguing in this stage of love is around trust and one question: Will you be there for me if I need you? This can look like many other questions: Will you be sexually faithful? Will you take care of me if I'm sick? How important am I to you? Can I trust you to do what you say you are going to do, and keep commitments? These questions, and arguments about these questions, are all precursors to having children. Because no cavewoman ever wanted to sit in her cave with the baby and wonder if the man was really going to bring back meat to feed the family, and no caveman ever wanted to come back to the cave after a long day of hunting prey to find another man tending his fire.

So stage two is about building trust, and stage three is about building loyalty. When you are in the third stage of love, you've chosen commitment. You know that this woman is the woman for you—it's an amazing choice to make, but it also means that you're vulnerable and you can get hurt. In this stage, you've chosen to go down the rabbit hole with your partner and to take an amazing journey together. You are commited to another person's well-being as much as you are committed to your own. This is powerful, and it goes both ways. Each of the stages of love is selective, and this third stage only works out if you are both committed to monogamy and mutual sacrifice for one another. If you are not monogamous in this stage, you open the door to experiencing limerence (stage one) love with another person. Those cocktails are powerful! In stage three, you still have oxytocin flowing when you have an orgasm and when you show affection to one another, and this keeps you bonded, but the rest of the chemicals in the cascade quiet down. Any other relationship choice besides monogamy during stage two is a big threat to this primary relationship and will keep you from entering stage three. We are not saying "plural love" (polyamory) can never work, but the chemicals and hormones of romantic love are highly focused and highly selective.

There are couples who made the choice to be committed and to marry, but who never went through all the stages of love, including the limerence phase. We found in our research that the couples we worked with who never "fell in love" always wondered if they had made the right choice and always felt like something was missing in their relationship.

Couples in stage three of love, we have found, always seem to feel there is a purpose to their relationship—that together they have created something bigger than themselves. And when these couples talk about meeting, falling in love, and choosing to be committed to each other, there are always expressions of fondness and admiration. They have a certain kind of ease with each other and an ability to talk to and confide in each other. They have created a sense of shared meaning and purpose in their lives. There is trust and loyalty. These are the hallmarks of commitment, and when a woman wants a commitment, this is what she is looking for. And it's what you should look for in the woman you choose to be committed to. Now, not all commitments lead to marriage and a lifetime together, but we believe, and the research shows, that men are happier, healthier, make more money, and live longer when they are married. We're not telling you to get married as a preventative health measure, but we know—from personal experience and from the research—that a deep, stage-three committed relationship with an incredible woman is deeply satisfying on every level. For gay men, the same is true about having a stage-three committed relationship with an incredible man. A man becomes his best self when he has a real partner in life at his side.

What do you get when you give up the possibility of sleeping with any woman who crosses your path? A lifetime of love and happiness, if you're willing to work at it. Nothing more. Nothing less.

But How Do I Know for Sure?

This love and commitment business can be tricky. We've talked about the physical components of the three stages of love, but what will it feel like and how will you know for sure she is the one for you?

There may be 10,000 women on the planet with whom you can have a really satisfying lifelong love relationship. So there's not "the one," but many potential ones. What we've found from decades of studying real-life couples in the Lab is that if she makes you feel insecure, or not quite good enough, or not attractive and desirable, or rejected and pushed away, or just plain bad about yourself—she's not one of the ones for you. If she makes you feel wonderful, if you feel desired, attractive, funny, and all-around wonderful, then she is one of your potential ones. And the same goes for how you make her feel about herself. Remember this. And when you are with her, if you feel like you are home—then she is the one for you. When a woman is the right woman for you, you feel comfortable and relaxed, like you are in a warm bed that was built just for you. If every time you are together things are negative and the bed feels icy cold with scratchy sheets, then she is probably not the one. A good relationship is not one where the negativity only increases. Sure, there will be conflict that you have to work through, but when a woman is the right woman, you will feel like your best self—more alive, more joyful, more adventurous. If it's not the right relationship there will be feelings of anger, helplessness, and perhaps even a tendency toward substance abuse and addiction. You feel like your worst self if she's not the one.

One of the important myths to dispel is the belief that you will feel completely compatible and alike in every area—you'll have the same hobbies, the same likes and dislikes, the same politics. Our research has shown that compatibility of similar interests are mostly irrelevant. What's more important is, what is it like to be together? You may both claim to love to kayak, but if you're arguing going down a river, then it doesn't matter that kayaking is a common interest.

The norm is that you won't be exactly alike, and this is a good thing. Men and women get to learn a lot from their differences. But there is one arena where compatibility is very important—feelings. How do you both relate to anger, sadness, fear, and joy? How do you express affection and love? If you have very different feelings about feelings, it can cause lots of trouble and lots of work (to make the relationship work).

We call this a metaemotion mismatch. If one of you avoids expressing feelings, avoids conflict, or is just uncomfortable with emotion expression in general, there is going to be trouble if the other person is more volatile and loves passionate and intense expressions of emotion. If you are mismatched, one partner is going to feel like the other partner is too intense, and one is going to feel like the other is too distant and cold. This combination rarely works out, especially when it comes to affection. Affection is an emotional need, and if you grew up in a family that didn't show affection or express emotion and she is someone who enjoys touch and affectionate gestures, this is going to be a problem and require work. The same is true if you have very different ways of experiencing and expressing anger, sadness, and fear.

The only other truly make-or-break issue in determining if she's the one is the issue of children. We'll discuss women and children in the next chapter, but if she has a completely opposite view of children (one of you wants them, one of you doesn't), then she is most likely not the one.

Make a Commitment—Live Longer

If you're like most men, you think you can ensure your longevity by eating right, working out at the gym, and watching your weight. But research shows that taking the same amount of time and investing it in connecting emotionally with the people closest to you in life, especially with the woman in your life, is what really ensures your health and a long life. A great relationship with a woman is really the best form of self-interest.

And the interesting fact is that it is marriage, not living together, that gives you the most health and longevity benefits. At some point you may have said, "Marriage is just a piece of paper.

I don't need that to be committed." But this is not what the research shows. Now part of this may have to do with who chooses to live together and who chooses to marry. Research shows that you can predict who will live together rather than get married based on high school records. Studies have found that people who live together have lower grades in high school, get into more trouble in high school, and are more likely to use alcohol, be promiscuous, and drive when drunk. None of these things lead to a longer life. In the book *American Couples*, authors Pepper Schwartz and Philip Blumstein studied more than 12,000 heterosexual cohabiters, same-sex couples, and married couples.[1] What they found surprised them. They expected that people who lived together would become more similar to married couples the longer they lived together. (Even our US laws say that after 7 years of cohabitation you're essentially married.) But what they found in their American sample was that the opposite was true: The longer a couple cohabited, the less they looked like a married couple when it came to commitment. And we're not just talking about sexual fidelity. Cohabiters were less likely to support each other during times of financial trouble or to be there for any kind of trouble. Cohabiters were also more likely to leave if someone better came along. In other words, there was a lack of commitment or way less commitment among those who were living together rather than married.

The type of commitment that comes with being married adds an average of 8 years to a man's life. The bottom line then, for men, is that a major key to longevity and good health is a quality committed relationship with a woman, and finding an educated woman is better than an uneducated woman, when it comes to health.

In the past 40 years in the United States, the number of men and women going to college after high school has soared. Now close to 70 percent of high school graduates attend college.

Research indicates that increased education and increased social status have health-giving effects. For example, a large Norwegian study of 20,000 married men ages 35 to 56, monitored from 1977 to 1992, found that education (particularly the wife's) had significant positive effects on the cardiovascular health of men.[2]

In the Norwegian study, in addition to men being less overweight and smoking less, having an educated wife was also more likely to result in the men having lower blood pressure and lower cholesterol. Sociologist Linda Waite claims in her book, *The Case for Marriage,* that one of the real reasons the benefits of marriage are so great for men is because single men take such terrible care of themselves.[3] She's right. When men are single, they tend to drift into bad health, and they're also more likely to become socially isolated. Men drink more when they're single. They use drugs more frequently. It's not the same for single women—they tend to lead pretty healthy lives without men.

University of Michigan psychologist James House, PhD, published a paper in the journal *Science* that showed that, across the planet, men who are socially isolated die young.[4] For many men, being connected to a woman guarantees that they will have an active and healthy social life and that they will be healthier than if they were single.

If that's not an incentive to find "the one," we don't know what is.

Commitment As a Journey

You can define commitment as *wanting* a relationship to last and *doing* what it takes to make the relationship last. When you commit, you say "This is the woman for me, this is my journey, and this is my path." When you find "the one," you cherish her and you express gratitude for what she adds to your life. You don't compare your relationship with her to what you might be missing out on by being committed. It's more than just trust and loyalty, it's an epic journey—the Hero's journey.

You make the decision to take this journey, and it can be risky. You are saying that this relationship, this one woman, is where you are going to get your needs met. You are vowing to be in this relationship no matter what and to weather any storm together. You are agreeing to build a life with this woman, love her for exactly who she is, and support her in becoming who she wants to be.

This is the Hero's journey when he makes a commitment. The Zero's journey is to always say, "Maybe there's something better out there. Why should I commit?" If you've found the one, cherish her, attune to her, make love to her, commit to her, and be there for her. You'll be absolutely amazed at how wonderful life can be.

For us, this knowledge is personal. We've been on our journeys for decades, and life has surpassed our wildest dreams.

CHEAT SHEET *for* HEROES

- ★ Men want commitment just as much as women do.
- ★ Most men know when a woman is "the one." There has to be an inherent rightness for a woman to be the one—she has to smell right, feel right, taste right, and look right.
- ★ There are three stages of love, and the stages are very selective. You can't just fall in love with anyone, and you can't make it work with everyone.
- ★ Stage one (limerence) usually lasts a few months and is not the time to decide if a woman is the one.
- ★ Stage two is about trust and knowing if you'll be there for each other.
- ★ The third stage of love is about loyalty and commitment.
- ★ Married men live longer, make more money, and are healthier than men who choose to live with a woman but stay unmarried.
- ★ You don't need to have similar likes and dislikes to work as a couple, but you do need to be compatible in how you handle conflict and express emotions and affection.
- ★ You will know she's the one if she makes you feel like you are your best self, and you feel more alive, adventurous, joyful, and loved when you are with her.
- ★ Finding the one and making a commitment are about doing what it takes to make a relationship last.

YOU MIGHT BE A ZERO IF . . .

- ✖ You refuse to ever commit.
- ✖ You think every woman is "the one."
- ✖ You make a commitment to a woman and don't honor it.
- ✖ You threaten to leave the relationship or bring up divorce when you are upset or in conflict.
- ✖ You don't cherish the woman in your life.
- ✖ You always think there might be something better out there than the woman you've committed to.
- ✖ You don't sacrifice for the relationship.
- ✖ You don't look to your relationship as the place to get your needs met.

Chapter 14

MOTHER NATURE

Understanding
Women and Children

Motherhood: All love begins and ends there.

—Robert Browning

JOHN QUINN HAD a problem. His wife was in labor and the hospital in Arcata, California, wouldn't allow him to be in the delivery room. He told the obstetrician simply, "This is my wife. I love her. I want to be there." The doctor said no, and hospital administrators claimed it wasn't safe to have him in the room, that they weren't set up for "spectators," and that it was "impossible."

John did what any 23-year-old college student in 1960 might have done in the face of injustice and tyranny—he protested, and through a single act of civil disobedience made headlines across a nation. So what did this young husband and soon-to-be-new-father do? He took a heavy metal chain, held his wife's hand in his, and wrapped the chain around both their wrists. He then attached two heavy padlocks. The only way he was leaving the delivery room was if the hospital removed both of them. The couple's baby boy was on his way, so the hospital staff called the

Woman Gives Birth To Son While Chained To Husband

College Student Padlocks Self To Wife After Being Denied Entry To Delivery Room

police but in the end they had no choice but to deliver the baby with John Quinn at his wife's side in the delivery room.

After the birth, John unlocked himself from his wife and walked calmly out of the room and past the hospital officials and police waiting outside. Newspaper reports say the police officer was "scratching his head" as John walked past. No charges were filed.

John Quinn is a Hero.

Four years later, in New Jersey, John Keim wasn't so lucky. In 1964, it was legal in California for a father to be in the delivery room, but that law hadn't made its way to New Jersey. John Keim, however, still refused to leave his wife's side as she gave birth to their second child. He ended up being arrested, charged with disorderly conduct, and fined $150. That may all seem like a long time ago, but even up until the mid-1980s it was illegal for a man to be at the delivery of his child unless he was married to the mother.

Today, in the United States, 91 percent of men are present at the births of their children. These men are also Heroes. They understand, just as John Quinn and John Keim understood, how important it is to support a woman's journey into and through motherhood. It's important to the woman, it's important to the child, and if you want to love a woman for a lifetime, it should be important to you.

By staking their claims in the delivery room, John Quinn and John Keim started an avalanche. Men are now a force to be reckoned with in the delivery room and are working alongside mothers as advocates and partners in the birth of children.

And it matters. Being present at the birth of a child has a huge effect on a man and on his relationship. Research shows that men who were present at the deliveries of their children are much nicer to their wives during disagreements than men who did not witness the births of their children. After witnessing Julie and Rachel give birth, John and Doug bow in their general direction. The force of nature that is a woman giving birth is awesome to behold.

How you support a woman during pregnancy and childbirth can have a huge impact on your relationship (and on your baby's development) 5, 10, and even 20 years down the road. You don't need to handcuff yourself to your wife physically, but you do need to attune emotionally. This makes all the difference.

Time to Grow Up

We know it can be hard. When you become a father for the first time you lose sleep, you lose freedom, and suddenly the woman you love has fallen in love with someone else. That someone else cries all the time, needs to be constantly held, and has even worse bathroom habits than you do—but she loves this little human in a way that is deep, sacred, and—most importantly—not to be messed with. It gives her superhuman strength. Superhuman instincts. And it gives her a superhuman drive to connect and protect.

Women have a biological investment in their offspring and an imperative to have their children survive. This has been true since the dawn of time. She is going to move heaven and hell to make sure her children survive, thrive, and have everything they need. You can understand, or you can get the hell out of her way. It's as simple as that.

Fortunately, if it is your child or one you have come to love, you may feel similarly.

Some men go through feelings of being left out, of not being important any longer, or of feeling like they're competing with a baby or children for their partner's time and attention. Men don't always admit these feelings out loud, but they can be there just the same. Remember that attachment and love hormone, oxytocin? It's powerful. And each time your partner holds your baby, cuddles your baby, nurses your baby, looks into your baby's eyes, tenderly touches your baby, or even smells your baby, her oxytocin levels increase. She's bonding with her infant, and it's how our species survives and children thrive.

If you find your feelings are hurt because suddenly she's not cuddling you, touching you, or obsessively sniffing the top of your head, it's understandable—common, in fact. And the only solution is to develop your own bond with the baby. Because what she needs most is your true partnership in raising the baby. Her need for you (no matter how much she loves, adores, or is obsessed with her little bundle) is as great, if not greater, than ever. And that little bundle needs you as well.

The Motherhood Constellation

The late psychiatrist Daniel Stern, MD, explained that when women are pregnant they begin to form a matrix around themselves of people who will support, encourage, and validate their new role and maternal identity.[1] Their sense of self becomes oriented toward their connection with their child and that child's well-being and safety. The motherhood constellation, where a woman is preoccupied with her child, Stern says, can last for years and become reactivated any time her child is in danger. As a father, you are part of this constellation—a big part of it. This motherhood constellation is critical to the child's development, and your role as father is also critical.

The bottom line is that a man who does not understand a woman's relationship with her children will never understand her. Whether the children are your own or not, you must understand the unique relationship that a woman has with her children. If you can't understand this part of her identity and her love, you will not understand a big part of her heart. One of the key ways that a man can love a woman is by supporting her role as a mother, loving her, and loving and nurturing her children.

Men Matter

More and more men are taking active roles in nurturing their babies or children. An increasing number are equal or primary caregivers, often being the one to stay home with a child. This is a big shift over the last few decades. When Rachel was in medical residency and Doug was the primary parent, there were very few dads who were caregivers. At the playgrounds, mothers would raise their eyebrows with suspicion, wondering who the strange man with the toddler was. Fortunately, this is no longer the case.

When fathers nurture their children, they don't have to try to be Mr. Moms. Historically, they have always had their own distinctive and very important ways of relating to children. When fathers nurture children, it has huge benefits.

If there is one thing that guys excel at, it is play. There are huge differences in how men and women play with babies. A father's play with a baby is more physical and tactile, while a mother's play is more visual and verbal. Author and pediatrician T. Berry Brazelton, MD, puts it this way: "mothers stroke, fathers poke." A father's play has fits and starts, because let's face it, if men are playing, they want it to be fun. If something isn't fun, they will stop and start something new every time.

In our Love Lab videos, we saw that women will persist in showing a baby some picture they think is important for the baby. "Here's the giraffe. The giraffe is the tallest animal in the zoo." Even if the baby crawls away, the mom will persist in showing the picture of the giraffe to the baby. For example, "Who is the tallest in the zoo?" said one mom to a 7-month-old baby as she showed him the picture of a giraffe. He crawled away. He didn't care about the giraffe. She circled around him and showed him the picture again. "Who is the tallest in the zoo?" And again he crawled away. Mom was relentless. She tried again, even as the baby again retreated. Mom is a baby's patient teacher.

Dads, on the other hand, will drop a game like a hot potato if the baby isn't interested. If they see the baby looking at a toy truck on the floor, dads start making truck sounds, "Chug, chug, chug, rumm, rummm, rummmm!" The baby is automatically captivated, and the dad *becomes the truck.* Guys are like another kid, and this isn't a patronizing thing. This is something that is critical to the baby's development and even critical to a man's relationship with his partner. Studies show that two-thirds of 2½-year-olds choose dads over moms as play partners. A father will shift games repeatedly with a baby or child if the child gets bored (or if dad gets bored), and it's like a roller-coaster ride for the baby. The baby gets disappointed when the first game ends, but then dad starts a new, even more exciting game. And in this process, babies learn to self-regulate. It's critical for their development, and this makes dads' high-speed, hyperactive, goofy way of playing extremely important. While moms are teachers, dads are guides. And babies need both. Hundreds of studies have proven that the way dads play is linked to major positive outcomes for both sons and daughters, both in intellectual and social development. And no one is more surprised by this than expectant fathers. That's why we tell expectant moms to be sure to include dad. Diapering and bathing a baby are daily events filled with the potential for great bouts of fun and play. Nothing is more fascinating to a baby than a father's (or mother's) face and voice.

Research reveals that fathers offer infants more freedom to explore, while moms promote more caution. Typically a father will encourage his very small child to climb even higher on the jungle gym. He may encourage this by being above his child instead of hovering around below, like the mother, who positions herself to catch the child if he or she falls.

Robert Sears, PhD, a Stanford psychologist, did research on 300 families when the children were 5 years old. Twenty-six years later, researchers Richard Koestner, PhD, Carol Franz, PhD, and Joel Weinberger, PhD, assessed the level of empathy in these same children, now young adults. They looked back at the child data to see what predicted their ability to be empathic when they were in their early thirties. Guess what: The best predictor of the empathy of the child was how involved the dad was when the child was 5 years old. The more involved the dads, the more empathic the kids.

In another follow-up study, Dr. Franz, Dr. Weinberger, and David McClelland, PhD, from Harvard University studied these people again when they were 41 years old. Those who had better social relationships in midlife (involving marriage, kids, and community) were those who experienced increased warmth from their dads when they were children.[2]

As we said earlier, there are literally hundreds of studies showing that a dad's playfulness and care are real assets for kids. Child development expert and University of Michigan Professor Norma Radin, PhD, was one of the first researchers to study the influence fathers have on the intellectual and emotional development of children. She reported that children who had actively involved fathers had higher verbal ability test scores.[3] Kevin Nugent, PhD, a longtime researcher and colleague of pediatrician Dr. Brazelton, reported that fathers' levels of caregiving during their infants' first years predicted infant IQ test scores. Fathers' skills as playmates (at things like peekaboo, ball toss, and bouncing) were related to having more intellectually advanced children.[4] Psychologists Robert Blanchard, PhD, and Henry Biller, PhD, found that underachieving third-grade boys, all with average IQs from working-class and middle-class homes, came from homes where the father had left before the child was 5 years old. Superior performers were those whose fathers were present and available to them. Fathers can be "absent" even in intact families. The nature of a dad's emotional presence matters a great deal. Biller and Blanchard reported that kids who had the hardest time with both social relationships and grades had fathers who were cold, authoritarian, derogatory, and intrusive.[5] And children aren't the only ones who benefit from active, involved fathers. Researchers and authors Rosalind Barnett, PhD, and Caryl Rivers, a professor of journalism at Boston University, found that wives are happier with their marriages and their own parenting when dads are around. They also found that men are happier in their relationships or marriages when child care and child rearing are shared.[6]

So the bottom line, when it comes to understanding women and children, is that you must understand how important a role you play as a father. A child will be much happier and healthier if you are a big part of the equation. And your relationship with your partner will also be happier and healthier.

You Are in This Together

Much has been written about the demands of motherhood on women, and it's good for you to offer understanding and support through all the phases of motherhood—from pregnancy through when the kids go off to college. There is not a lot of talk, however, about how many men feel overwhelmed by the demands of being in a relationship, running a household, being successful in their careers, helping take care of children, and trying to satisfy all their partners' needs.

Before the days of no-fault divorce, many men who were burdened by families simply disappeared. They abandoned their homes, their wives, and their children, and they simply went out for a pack of cigarettes or a carton of milk and never returned. Where did they go? Many of these men set up new identities and started all over again. They thought a fresh start would simply hit the reset button.

There is still that sense in many guys of being overwhelmed by all the demands of family life. At times, everyone in a relationship wants to bail and hit that reset button. This feeling is related to "running on empty." Many men that John and Julie see in therapy are running on empty. When children become part of the equation, men complain that their lives don't have enough fun, playfulness, good sex, or adventure. They complain that women are just too involved with the minutiae of daily living and, especially when children arrive, that their lives become an endless to-do list. There's no fun, no romance, no passion, no adventure.

This doesn't have to be the case, and men are the critical factor when it comes to making a family life and a romantic life that continues to be fun, adventurous, and a true partnership. Yes, there are more demands on your time when a child or children enter the picture, but you can fight it or you can roll up your sleeves and become a partner in this wild and fabulous adventure called family life. As John and Doug and many other men who have had the joy and privilege of being caregivers for children believe, there is actually nothing in life more rewarding. If you win a Nobel Prize or sell a start-up for a billion dollars, it will pale in comparison to the love and satisfaction that comes from helping your children grow up. The truth is, mother love is a force of nature—and so is father love. As we explained earlier, men are the crucial variable in the success or failure of relationships. They are also a crucial variable in the success of a family.

★ If you want to truly understand a woman, you have to understand and support her role as a mother. She has a biological drive to bond with her child and ensure her child's survival. This isn't about her not loving you or you not being as important to her.

★ As a woman becomes a mother, she needs you more than ever, and your support during this transition is critical to the health of your relationship.

★ Men play a critical role in a child's development—dad's playtime with a baby or child leads to the child having a higher IQ, becoming a more empathic adult, and having happier and healthier relationships later in life. You matter a lot.

★ Whether you are the biological father or the father by marriage or choice, you are important to the health and well-being of your child or children.

★ If you are feeling left out after a new baby is born, talk to your partner about it.

★ It's up to you to ensure that the demands and workload of having a family are shared and equal. See family life as a great adventure and your relationship will thrive. You can keep the romance, flirtation, play, and adventure alive (and the conflict down) by sharing the workload and becoming her equal partner in the home, family, and relationship. Nurture your friendship and continue to attune.

YOU MIGHT BE A ZERO IF...

✖ Your partner is exhausted and needs your help and you don't take over or lend a hand when needed.

✖ You compete with the baby or children for attention.

✖ You exclude yourself or withdraw from family life.

✖ You don't play with your baby or child.

✖ You bail on the family physically or emotionally.

✖ You think it should be all about you, even after children enter the relationship.

✖ You are not kind to or respectful of your partner or her/your children.

✖ You comment about a woman's weight while she's pregnant or after the baby comes.

✖ You don't listen when your partner shares her concerns about being a mother or about your children's welfare.

✖ You don't talk to your partner if you are feeling left out or pushed aside after the birth of a baby.

Chapter 15

STAYING TOGETHER

Loving a Woman for a Lifetime

When you trip over love, it is easy to get up.

But when you fall in love, it is impossible to stand again.

—Albert Einstein

ALBERT EINSTEIN IS perhaps the greatest mind the world has ever known. His name is forever associated with genius, and upon his death his brain was removed and preserved so that some day neuroscience might be able to figure out why he was so smart. Yes, he developed the theory of relativity, but when it came to figuring out how to keep a woman for a lifetime, Einstein was just as clueless as most men. (As we saw at the very beginning of the book, the man who could explain the nature of the universe, Stephen Hawking, could not fathom the nature of women either.) In 1914, with his marriage falling apart, Einstein gave his wife, Mileva, a list of conditions she needed to follow if she wanted to stay with him.[1]

A. You will make sure:

　　1. that my clothes and laundry are kept in good order;

　　2. that I will receive my three meals regularly *in my room;*

3. that my bedroom and study are kept neat, and especially that my desk is left for *my use only.*

B. You will renounce all personal relations with me insofar as they are not completely necessary for social reasons. Specifically, you will forego:
   1. my sitting at home with you;
   2. my going out or travelling with you.

C. You will obey the following points in your relations with me:
   1. you will not expect any intimacy from me, nor will you reproach me in any way;
   2. you will stop talking to me if I request it;
   3. you will leave my bedroom or study immediately without protest if I request it.

D. You will undertake not to belittle me in front of our children, either through words or behavior.

Needless to say, a few months after being presented with this list, Mileva took their two children, left Einstein, and filed for divorce. She also, incidentally, received every last cent of his Nobel Prize money.

After all the hard work that's gone into meeting, dating, and deciding a woman is "the one," how do you keep her happy for a lifetime? How do you keep your relationship growing, evolving, and just as exciting after 10 years as it was after 10 days, after 5 decades as it was after 5 months? First and foremost, do not ever give her a list of demands that she has to follow in order to stay with you. (Unless, of course, you really like living alone.) The second most important thing is to never, ever think you know all there is to know about her. You can't. You don't. And what a Hero does that sets him apart from a Zero is to be endlessly curious about the interior world of his partner—her hopes, her fears, and her dreams.

We can't emphasize this enough.

Never stop dating her. Never stop getting to know her. Never stop connecting with her. Give her your attention, your time, and your support, and be there when she needs you. Listen to her. This is how you build trust, and it also doesn't hurt that listening is like Viagra for a woman. This is how you make her feel emotionally and physically safe. And this is how you keep her love.

And don't forget, you're going to have to keep sharing your interior world, as well. You are going to have to constantly be brave enough to be vulnerable. Whether your relationship lasts or doesn't is up to you. As we said in the beginning, *you are the make-or-break factor in your relationship.*

Make it, don't break it.

A Word about Trust

At first, it may seem obvious that trust is essential for a relationship to thrive, but we had no idea how absolutely central it is to the success and failure of all relationships. When we interviewed couples throughout the United States, from virtually every major socioeconomic and ethnic group, they mentioned trust again and again. Unhappy couples came right out and told us that trust was missing from their relationships; they simply could not count on their partners to "be there" for them when they needed them most. Over time, the emotional injuries they sustained from this lack of trust built a huge emotional gulf between them, damaging their marital friendship and killing off their love.

Couples whose relationships were successful said mutual trust made them feel safe with each other. It enabled them to be vulnerable and thereby deepen their love beyond that first passionate infatuation and courtship. Their sexual life flourished and increasingly became based on knowing and loving one another intimately and deeply. For them, trust was intertwined with a sense of safety and with loving and allowing friendship and intimacy to blossom.

Distrust and betrayal are at the heart of *every* failed relationship—even if there hasn't been an actual affair. This is true *even if the couple is unaware that distrust is their problem.* Distrust and betrayal don't only ruin relationships—they also have biological consequences that can literally kill you. The good news is that increasing the degree of trust in your relationship improves not only your love life but your health, as well.

What makes a relationship most vulnerable to betrayal is *avoiding* conflict and hiding parts of yourself so you don't "rock the boat." You may think it's just easier to not say anything when either one of you is upset, but research shows that when there is a gradual pattern of conflict avoidance, there is increased emotional distance in the relationship. When you have increased emotional distance, you are setting the conditions and the stage for an affair. Affairs can be physical, and affairs can be emotional. If you leave your partner feeling lonely day in and day out, eventually she's going to find someone else to fill the void. Either you turn toward her or she's going to turn toward someone else. And at the end of the day, in each interaction with your partner, you are either building trust and commitment or building a lack of commitment and eventual betrayal. Think about it. She's had an argument with her best friend and is upset. She tells you about it and you either attune and turn toward her with empathy or you turn on the television because you only want the kind of drama that comes with commercials. If you don't lend a shoulder to cry on or listen to her pain, a crack forms in the foundation of your relationship. Form enough cracks over time and the whole house will come crashing down. Betrayal doesn't just happen out of the blue—it is a long, slow, almost glacial slide built out of secrets, unexpressed feelings and needs, and moments of connection that were missed or dismissed. If you turn away from your partner enough times, she won't be there when you finally turn back.

In some ways, this book can be boiled down to a very simple mathematical equation:

Hero > Zero

WHY?

Hero = turns *toward* his Partner

Zero = turns *away from* his Partner

IT'S REALLY QUITE SIMPLE.

MOVE OVER, EINSTEIN.

Affair-Proofing Your Relationship

If you are going to affair-proof your relationship, you are going to invest in and commit to the relationship. You are not going to think you can do better than the woman you're with or that somewhere out there in the world is a woman who will love and adore you when you want her to, will leave you alone when you want her to, and won't expect you to meet any of her needs. This is Einstein's relationship theory of relativity. It didn't work for him, and it certainly won't work for you.

If you want to stay together, constantly build love and loyalty, and be the Hero in your partner's world, then you need to put energy into your relationship. Here are some guidelines to making love last.

"Yes, but how long will you *love me forever?*"

www.cartoonstock.com

THE 6-SECOND KISS. Every time you leave one another, whether it's to go to work, the grocery store, or the gym, kiss good-bye for 6 seconds. Not 1 second. Not 2 seconds. Six seconds. If you want to make out for 2 minutes, that's fine also, but the kiss needs to be at least 6 seconds long. The same goes for when you first see each other after being apart. Six seconds of kissing, every single time. When you were first together you kissed all the time, and there's no reason to ever stop kissing her. It builds romance. It builds passion. Why the 6-second kiss? The oxytocin starts flowing, and as we discussed earlier, fear lessens and trust is built.

DATE HER. Just because she now shares your mailbox doesn't mean dating should end. You've heard this before, but it really is sound advice: Make time at least once each week for a date night. Plan it. Prepare for it. Get excited for it, like it's the first time you dated. Think of new places to go, new things to experience, and make romancing her a habit. Court her and seduce her with the same energy you had at the beginning of your relationship. You can also get some more guidance from our book, *10 Dates: Conversations That Lead to a Lifetime of Love,* which all four of us wrote for couples to help them keep love alive and juicy.

GET TO KNOW HER. Remember when you could talk for hours and you never got tired of learning new things about each other? This doesn't have to end. There are still things to learn about her. Never stop being curious about your partner's inner world. Ask open-ended questions—questions that can't be answered by a yes or a no. Do you know what she would do if she won the lottery? What does she dream about? What and who are most important in her life right now? What is she afraid of? What is she worried about? What is she looking forward to? What is her biggest struggle? Having these conversations is a way of connecting and building trust, and that is the glue that keeps your relationship solid.

APPRECIATE HER. Find some way every day to show your appreciation and gratitude that this woman is in your life. Compliment her, thank her, admire her, show her with your words and your actions that you love and value her. Tell her she is beautiful. Let her know you desire her. Do something nice for her. It doesn't have to be elaborate; even emptying the dishwasher can show appreciation. These positive interactions are like money in the bank, and when you do something stupid (as all men inevitably do), she is going to be far more likely to forgive you and overlook your momentary lapse of sanity if you have a strong reserve in the positivity bank account.

HONOR HER DREAMS. Too often, women will put their own dreams aside for the sake of the family, or the relationship, or because we live in a society where a woman's dreams are not quite as important—especially if they don't involve being a wife or a mother. Everyone's dreams are important. Your dreams are important. Her dreams are important. And research shows that the longevity and success of a relationship depends on each person supporting the goals of the other person. If you don't honor your partner's dreams and do everything in your power to help her fulfill them, you will find yourself in a relationship with a woman who is depressed, defeated, and beaten down. Every man wants a relationship with a woman who is fully alive, who loves her life, and who is everything she dreams of being. If you don't know what her dreams are, ask. Then move mountains, if need be, to help her make them come true.

As we discussed in Chapter 1, in our Love Lab we found that women have two major complaints about men: (1) He's never there for me, and (2) there isn't enough intimacy and connection. There is nothing worse for a woman than being in a relationship and feeling lonely. You don't want this for the woman you love, and you have the power to prevent it by paying attention to her and to your relationship.

Life can be difficult, and research has investigated what factors are important when women face extreme life stress, such as coping with illness or death or other traumas. That research has shown that women, even women who are alone, cope well with extreme adversity when they honor their life dreams. That honoring becomes a wellspring for facing even severe adversity, for transcending disappointments and setbacks. By knowing and respecting their deepest aspirations, hopes, desires, and ambitions, they increase the probability of leading a fulfilling and creative life. But women need not face adversity alone if they have a man who accepts them and understands them deeply. When a woman is in a relationship with a partner who knows and honors her life dreams, she feels understood, respected, and deeply loved.

When she feels understood, respected, and deeply loved by you, then you have created a relationship and a love that will last. In the end, isn't this what you want? The love of a woman? To be desired and accepted by a woman? From that first awkward meeting to learning the intricacies of living with one another in a relationship, in the end, what men most want to know about women is how to love them and how to get their love in return.

Yes, your biology is different, your communication styles may be different, and your needs may be different, but ultimately men and women, as different as they are, want the same things in relationships—joy, intimacy, respect, understanding, better sex, more fun, and less conflict.

As gender roles have changed over the decades, men have been left somewhat confused about how to achieve these goals. Should they protect and provide, or should they nurture and care-take? Should they raise their status in the workforce or raise the children? Should they provide a strong shoulder or a sensitive ear?

In short, what the hell are men supposed to do?

In the end, all you can do is love the woman in your life. Cherish her. Embrace the ways she is different from you and learn from her. A guide to women is a guide to understanding yourself. You are at your best when you are in a loving, exciting, and life-changing relationship with a woman. They will challenge you. They will confuse you. They will sometimes break you, and they will heal you. The greatest mystery of all, when it comes to women, is not why they do what they do, but why men feel so much when they are with them. Women are a man's connection to the world and to life itself.

Let's face it: You may struggle at times to understand women, but understanding them, and loving them, is one of the greatest adventures life has to offer.

ACKNOWLEDGMENTS

We would first like to thank all of the men and women who participated in the Love Lab research and who shared their stories with us through our research and our clinical practices. We have been deeply privileged to hear what most women never say and what most men never hear. The research has given us a window into the hearts and minds, the joys and discontents that unfold over a lifetime of relationship, and we feel extremely grateful for the trust and generosity of these confidences.

We want to thank the team at Rodale who believed in and supported this book, including Jeff Csatari, who saw the potential of this book from the start, and Leah Miller, who has been a brilliant champion for the book, and her able assistant, Mollie Thomas. We would also like to thank the rest of the extraordinary team at Rodale, including Jennifer Levesque, Mary Ann Naples, and Maria Rodale. A great organization is always defined by superb leadership, and Rodale is blessed to have it in all three. They share skills, passion, and warmth, and it has been a joy working with them over the years.

We would like to thank our amazing teams at the Gottman Institute, at the Santa Cruz Integrative Medicine Center, and at Idea Architects. We feel enormously supported and grateful for their care, creativity, and kindness. But there is one person that we want to thank more than anyone, our literary collaborator and creative partner, Lara Love Hardin. This book would not have been possible without her great talents as a writer and her kickass sense of humor. Lara has a exceptional ability to take research, ideas, advice, and stories and to wave a magic wand over them in a way that brings them to life in fascinating and fun prose. We could not have been more fortunate to have her as part of our brain trust, our writing team, and our circle of friendship. The book you hold in your hands was only possible because of her extraordinary gift of self.

Finally, we would like to thank our children Moriah Gottman and Jesse, Kayla, and Eliana Carlton Abrams. May *The Man's Guide* help you and your generation, as well as the generations that follow, to find the key to unlock the love that you so richly deserve. We love you, and you are our inspiration in everything we do.

ENDNOTES

Chapter 1

1 National Fatherhood Initiative, "Statistics on the Father Absence Crisis in America," accessed June 1, 2015, fatherhood.org/media/consequences-of-father-absence-statistics.

2 Helen Fisher, PhD, "How to Build Intimacy In Your Relationship," October 2009, oprah.com/relationships/Building-Intimacy-Gender-Differences-in-Intimacy.

Chapter 2

1 G. Miller, J. M. Tybur, and B. D. Jordan, "Ovulatory cycle effects on tip earnings by lap dancers: Economic evidence for human estrus?" *Evolution & Human Behavior* 28, no. 6 (November 1, 2007): 375-81.

2. Loren McCarter and Robert W. Levenson, "Sex differences in physiological reactivity to the acoustic startle" (lecture, presented at Society for Psychophysiological Research Thirty-Eighth Annual Meeting, Hyatt Regency Denver, Colorado, September 23-27, 1998).

3. J. A. Coan, H. S. Schaefer, and R. J. Davidson, "Lending a hand: social regulation of the neural response to threat," *Psychological Science* 17, no. 12 (December 2006): 1032-9.

Chapter 3

1. J. Djordjevic, A. M. Toma, A. I. Zhurov, and S. Richmond, "Three-dimensional quantification of facial symmetry in adolescents using laser surface scanning," *European Journal of Orthodontics* 36, no. 2 (April 27, 2014): 125-32.

2. L. A. Renninger, T. J. Wade, K. Grammer, "Getting that female glance: Patterns and consequences of male nonverbal behavior in courtship contexts," *Evolution & Human Behavior* 25, no. 6 (November 2004): 416-31.

3. D. Archer, "The effects of timing of self-disclosure on attraction and reciprocity," *Journal of Personality and Social Psychology* 38 (1980): 120-30.

4. M. J. Rantala, et al., "Evidence for the stress-linked immunocompetence handicap hypothesis in humans," *Nature Communications* vol. 3, no. 694 (February 21, 2012): 10.1038/ncomms1696.

Chapter 4

1. J. Kellerman, J. Lewis, and J. D. Laird, "Looking and loving: The effects of mutual gaze on feelings of romantic love," *Journal of Research in Personality* 23, no. 2 (June 1989): 145-61. voiceresearch.org/publications

2. Ibid.

3. http://voiceresearch.org/publications.

4. Y. Xu, A. Lee, W-L. Wu, X. Liu, and P. Birkholz, "Human vocal attractiveness as signaled by body size projection," *PLoS ONE* 8, no. 4 (2013): e62397.

5. N. Guéguen, "Courtship compliance: The effect of touch on women's behavior," *Social Influence* 2, no. 2 (2007): 81-97.

6. R. D. Clark III and E. Hatfield, "Gender differences in receptivity to sexual offers," *Journal of Psychology & Human Sexuality* 2, no. 1 (1989): 39-55.

7. M. Voracek, A. Hofhansl, and M. L. Fisher, "Clark and Hatfield's evidence of women's low receptivity to male strangers' sexual offers revisited," *Psychological Reports* 97, no. 1 (August 2005): 11-20.

Chapter 5

1. Ivanka Savic, Hans Berglund, and Per Lindström, "Brain response to putative pheromones in homosexual men," *Proceedings of the National Academy of Sciences* 102, no. 20 (May 17, 2005): 7356-61.

2. Y. Martins, et al., "Preference for human body odors is influenced by gender and sexual orientation," *Psychological Science* 16 (2005): 694-701.

3. Christine Fisher, Karina Hamaouche, and Kendall Sauer, "Consistency of first kiss recall among couples: Evidence of collaborative recollection," (presentation, 23rd Annual Psychological Science Convention, Washington, DC, May 27, 2011: Sponsored by Butler University, Faculty Sponsor by John Bohannon).

4. S. M. Hughes, M. A. Harrison, and G. G. Galllup, Jr., "Sex differences in romantic kissing among college students: An evolutionary perspective," *Evolutionary Psychology* 5 (2007): 612-31.

Chapter 6

1. T. Baumgartner, et al., "Oxytocin shapes the neural circuitry of trust and trust adaptation in humans," *Neuron* 58, no. 4 (May 22, 2008): 639-50.

2. Jeffry A. Simpson, W. Andrew Collins, and Jessica E. Salvatore, "The impact of early interpersonal experience on adult romantic relationship functioning: Recent findings from the Minnesota longitudinal study of risk and adaptation," *Current Directions in Psychological Science* 20, no. 6 (December 2011): 355-59.

Chapter 7

1. Joni Johnstone, *Appearance Obsession: Learning to Love the Way You Look* (New York: Health Communications, 1994).

Chapter 8

1. E. Chack and A. Ellis, "Here's What Happens When You Ask a Bunch of Adults to Label Male and Female Reproductive Systems," BuzzFeed, March 10, 2014, buzzfeed.com/erinchack/heres-what-happens-when-you-ask-a -bunch-of-adults-to-label-m#.vxX3PIJBa.

Chapter 9

1. E. Sandra Byers and Larry Heinlein, "Predicting initiations and refusals of sexual activities in married and cohabiting heterosexual couples," *The Journal of Sex Research* 26, no. 2 (May 1989): 210-31.

2. Chrisanna Northrup, Pepper Schwartz, and James Witte, *The Normal Bar: The Surprising Secrets of Happy Couples and What They Reveal About Creating a New Normal in Your Relationship* (New York: Harmony, 2013).

Chapter 10

1. James R. Averill, "Studies on anger and aggression: Implications for theories of emotion," *American Psychologist* 38, no. 11 (November 1983): 1145-60.

2. S. P. Thomas, "Women's anger, aggression, and violence," *Health Care for Women International* 26, no. 6 (2005): 504-22.

Chapter 11

1. T. Heermann, "4 Gender Differences in Marketing Approach," Market It Write, September 9, 2012, marketitwrite.com/blog/ 2010/02/4-gender -differences-in-marketing-approach/.

2. O. N. Nelson, "Effect of gender on customer loyalty: A relationship marketing approach," *Marketing Intelligence & Planning* 24, no. 1 (2006): 48-61.

3. M. DeLacey, "Trying to Impress a Man? Steer Clear of the Sales," *Daily Mail*, July 5, 2013, dailymail.co.uk/femail/article-2356781 /Men-bored-just-26-MINUTES-shopping--women-2-hours.html.

4. P. M. Bentler and Michael D. Newcomb, "Longitudinal study of marital success and failure," *Journal of Consulting and Clinical Psychology* 46, no. 5 (September 1978): 1053-70.

Chapter 12

1. C. H. Kroenke, et al., "Social networks, social support, and survival after breast cancer diagnosis," *Journal of Clinical Oncology* 24, no. 7 (March 1, 2006): 1105-11.
2. L. F. Berkman and S. L. Syme, "Social networks, host resistance, and mortality: A nine-year follow-up study of alameda county residents," *American Journal of Epidemiology* 109, no. 2 (1979): 186-204.
3. R. Dunbar, *Grooming, Gossip, and the Evolution of Language* (Cambridge, MA: Harvard University Press, 1996).
4. R. W. Wrangham, "An ecological model of female-bonded primate groups," *Behaviour* 75 (1980): 262-300.
5. S. E. Taylor, et al., "Biobehavioral responses to stress in females: Tend-and-befriend, not fight-or-flight," *Psychological Review* 107, no. 3 (July 2000): 411-29.
6. Lois M. Verbrugge, "Marital status and health," *Journal of Marriage and the Family* 41, no. 2 (1979): 278.
7. M. Komarovsky, *Blue-Collar Marriage* (New Haven, CT: Yale University Press, 1987).

Chapter 13

1 P. Blumstein and P. Schwartz, *American Couples* (New York: William Morrow & Co. 1999).
2. Grace M. Egelanda, Aage Tverdala, Haakon E. Meyera, and Randi Selmera, "A man's heart and a wife's education: A 12-year coronary heart disease mortality follow-up in Norwegian men," *International Journal of Epidemiology* 31, no. 4 (2002): 799-805.
3 Linda Waite, *The Case for Marriage: Why Married People are Happier, Healthier and Better Off Financially* (New York: Broadway Books, 2001).
4 J. S. House, K. R. Landis, and D. Umberson, "Social relationships and health," *Science* 241 (July 29, 1988): 540-45.

Chapter 14

1 Daniel Stern, MD, *The Motherhood Constellation* (London: Basic Books, 1995).

2. Carol E. Franz, David C. McClelland, and Joel Weinberger, "Childhood antecedents of conventional social accomplishment in midlife adults: A 36-year prospective study," *Journal of Personality and Social Psychology* 60, no. 4 (April 1991): 586-95.

3   E. Williams and N. Radin, "Effects of father participation in child rearing," *American Journal of Orthopsychiatry* 69, no. 3 (July 1999): 328-36, http://faculty.mwsu.edu/psychology/dave.carlston/Writing%20 in%20Psychology/Fathering/4/williams.pdf.

4   J. K. Nugent, "Cultural and psychological influences on the father's role in infant development," *Journal of Marriage and the Family* 53, (1991): 475-585.

5   Henry B. Biller, *Fathers and Families: Paternal Factors in Child Development* (Santa Barbara, CA: Praeger, 1993).

6   R. C. Barnett and C. Rivers, *She Works/He Works: How Two-Income Families Are Happier, Healthier and Better Off* (Cambridge, MA: Harvard University Press, 1998).

Chapter 15

1   Walter Isaacson, *Einstein: His Life and Universe* (New York: Simon & Schuster, 2007).

INDEX

Underscored page references indicate sidebars. **Boldface** references indicate illustrations.

ABOUT THE AUTHORS

John Gottman, PhD

World-renowned for his work on marital stability and divorce prediction, Dr. John Gottman has conducted 40 years of breakthrough research with thousands of couples. He is a professor emeritus of psychology at the University of Washington, where he founded the world famous "Love Lab." The Love Lab is profiled extensively in Malcolm Gladwell's book, *Blink*. He is co-founder of The Gottman Institute and is also the Executive Director of the affiliated Relationship Research Institute. His work has earned him numerous major awards, including four National Institute of Mental Health Research Scientist Awards and the American Psychological Association's Presidential Citation for Outstanding Lifetime Research Contribution.

Dr. Gottman is also the author of 200 published academic articles and author or co-author of 42 books including *The New York Times* bestseller *The Seven Principles for Making Marriage Work*. He has appeared on numerous TV programs, including *Good Morning America*, the *Today* show, *CBS Morning News*, and *Oprah*. *Psychotherapy Networker* has voted him as one of the Top 10 Most Influential Therapists of the past quarter-century.

Julie Schwartz Gottman, PhD

Dr. Julie Schwartz Gottman is the co-founder and president of The Gottman Institute. She is also the co-creator of the immensely popular The Art and Science of Love weekend workshops for couples, and co-designer of the clinical training program in Gottman Method Couples Therapy, which she has taught in over a dozen countries worldwide. Dr. Schwartz Gottman is widely recognized for her clinical psychotherapy treatment, with specialization in distressed couples, abuse and trauma survivors, substance abusers and their partners, and cancer patients and their families.

She is the author or co-author of four books: *Ten Lessons to Transform Your Marriage*, *And Baby Makes Three*, *The Marriage Clinic Casebook*, and *Ten*

Principles for Doing Effective Couples Therapy. Dr. Schwartz Gottman was voted Washington State Psychologist of the Year in 2002.

Douglas Abrams

Douglas Abrams is a former editor at the University of California Press and HarperCollins. He is the founder of Idea Architects, a book and media development agency, which works with visionary authors to create a wiser, healthier, and more just world. In his life and work, he is interested in cultivating all aspects of our humanity: body, emotions, mind, and spirit.

He is the co-author of a number of bestselling books on love, sexuality, and spirituality, including books written with Archbishop Desmond Tutu, Yogacharya B.K.S. Iyengar, and Taoist Master Mantak Chia. His books with Mantak Chia include *The Multi-Orgasmic Man* and *The Multi-Orgasmic Couple.* He has also written two novels, *The Lost Diary of Don Juan* and *Eye of the Whale,* both of which were *San Francisco Chronicle* bestsellers. These novels have been published in over thirty languages. He lives with his wife, Rachel, a family physician, and their three children, Jesse, Kayla, and Eliana, in Santa Cruz, California.

Rachel Carlton Abrams, MD

Rachel Carlton Abrams, MD, MHS, received her medical degree at the University of California San Francisco and a master's degree in Holistic Health and Medical Sciences from the University of California Berkeley. She is board certified in both Family Medicine and Integrative and Holistic Medicine. She served on the board of the American Holistic Medical Association and runs an integrative medicine clinic in Santa Cruz, California.

Dr. Carlton Abrams has published two books on holistic health and sexuality, *The Multi-Orgasmic Woman* and *The Multi-Orgasmic Couple.* She has taught workshops regularly at Esalen Institute and throughout the country on relationships, sexuality, and holistic health. Her forthcoming book is entitled *BodyWise: Discovering Your Body's Intelligence for Lifelong Health and Healing.*